# CULTIVATED

# Cultivated

The Elements of Floral Style

CHRISTIN GEALL

PRINCETON ARCHITECTURAL PRESS • NEW YORK

# Contents

# Introduction

*You have no idea how wonderful it is to come out of the dark frustration of being unable to crystallize such visions as you may have, and to find suddenly a possible medium of expression.*
—CONSTANCE SPRY

One of the happiest moments of my life took place in an abandoned building in Scotland. The building was an old stone shed built into a wall—a wall surrounding an Edwardian garden at the Cambo Estate. The slate roof was barely intact, the floor dirt. My only company? Pigeons.

I'd been drawn to the building because of the light. It came in from one side, intimate but vast, like Vermeer's, illuminating a small interior space with a doorway cut into one wall.

That I saw that light and understood its potential is magical to me in retrospect, but what I created in that shed changed me forever.

You see, I haven't always been an artist, let alone a photographer. At the time, I was a gardener, mother, writer, and professor. While some might say I'm a creative person, that creativity had been cultivated on a dilettante's schedule. After a double major in environmental studies and anthropology, I'd trained in herbalism in the United States then horticulture at Kew Gardens in England, but later I went on to study writing in graduate school then a bit of painting, color theory, and art history. Like a magpie drawn to one shiny object after another, I flitted from subject to subject, staying loyal only to two sanity savers—writing and gardening.

If you'd asked me at the time what I was doing in that shed in Scotland, the professor in me would have had an answer, but I myself might not have believed it: I was serving as a florist in residence on the estate.

What does such a person do? I didn't know entirely, even after I pitched the idea to the owners and head gardener. They just let me get on with it, assuming I knew what "it" was. So I roamed around with a borrowed bucket and wheelbarrow looking for flowers to pick in the dark days of October. I begged vessels and an old folding card table from the house manager. I tried to put together color palettes. I sought out places to photograph my arrangements. And I silently questioned my every move.

One thing in my favor: I knew plants. I'd spent thirty years learning about them, growing them, selling them, and loving them. But at that time I knew I wasn't truly a florist, nor did I want solely to be one. I wanted in that moment what my writing peers got from their residencies—time to work, a change of scene, and an acknowledgment of my craft. I was a beginner, and, like many beginners, I was talking the talk and banking heavily on luck.

So I made a deal with myself to do at least one arrangement a day, no matter what, and photograph it as best I could. I had no tripod, so most of my pictures were blurry, and because of the latitude and time of year, there was very little light. I had no idea where my designs might take me from one day to the next, but no matter what, I got started. And that starting, that instinct to begin with doubt, is what matters most.

Floral design is about using what you have to the best of your ability within your time constraints and the limitations of the plants before you. It's about not knowing where you will end up. The same could be said of writing—and has been by Annie Dillard: "When you write, you lay down a line of words. The line of words is a miner's pick, a woodcarver's gouge, a surgeon's probe. You wield it, and it digs a path you follow."

Learning photography is no different: you learn how to best capture an image by choosing to take that first look through the lens.

That's predominantly what this book is about—discovering how to see flowers. My magpie tendencies have thankfully suited me well; in this book you'll find color theory and discussions of fashion, form, and style but also ruminations on gardening and seasonality that I feel are fundamental to an appreciation of the art. This book is both an aesthetic and personal inquiry—an exploration of history, culture, the senses, and my own understanding, which I hope might serve as tools for interpreting and appreciating floral design in new ways.

You'll find that much of the text acts as a guide to the images. This is a pedagogical approach adapted from the fine arts—to borrow from the painter Kit White, providing an apposite image is a way to bridge thought and embodiment. First, look at the work before you. Then read, learn, and interpret anew.

As such, this is not a how-to or recipe book. My process has been one of learning little truths about light and color and form and style as I've done the work. You'll discover tips on floral design and on how to grow and work with specific flowers, of course, but I also hope you'll gain the language to describe, appreciate, and expand your design work and relationship to plants.

Now, back to the shed. At the moment I took this picture, I had a piece of music in my mind that to this day makes me happy. It's the theme song from a somewhat cheesy movie I watched on my transatlantic flight to Scotland, the final scene of which instigated one of those uniquely low-oxygen time-smeared epiphanies that had me in tears.

The title of the movie, *A Little Chaos,* was fitting enough for what I was doing in that shed—arranging perennials in the gloaming, yearning to make something beautiful, trying to capture the romance of the place through flowers. But once dusk had truly fallen and I was forced to give up, I returned to my room in the clock tower and learned more about the music.

It had been composed by a young Scottish cellist, Peter Gregson, hired by Alan Rickman, who directed and acted in the film. In the final scene, as the title track plays, Rickman steps into a moment of his own creation, into a garden. It's known as the Bosquet de la Salle de Bal, and over the course of the film we witness its hard-wrought construction at Versailles. In that last scene, as violins and cellos begin to sing, we see the garden's designer (played by Kate Winslet) shift from trepidation to pride as Rickman, playing Louis XIV, enters the sunken garden for the first time. Water cascades from tiers of shells, musicians lean into their instruments, and people dance in a swirl of silk while Rickman stands still, a center point of awe, glory, and magnificence.

In that lonely clock tower room on the Scottish estate, I edited my pictures and listened to "A Little Chaos" over and over again. I sent Peter Gregson the picture I'd taken that day, and he, oddly, miraculously, and kindly, replied. Then I, too, danced and swirled solo that night, knowing I'd made something good that day. No matter how small, ephemeral, and imperfect, it was done: I'd made nature into art and found a new confidence in myself in the process.

I wish the same for you after reading this book—the delight of creation blooming in your chest. You don't need a cello, but I hope as you work with flowers, you might just feel one playing in your heart.

# PART ONE

# FINDING FLOWERS AND PLANTS

# Conveying a Sense of Place

My garden directs my designs. You could say I'm privileged in that regard, but utter that word to me on a grim November day, with my boots squelching through mud as I stuff tulip bulbs into heavy earth, and I might bluster: "Growing your own flowers is a hell of a lot of work."

So don't. Buy them. Sashay down to the bodega, grab a few bunches of brightly colored beauties, and put them to work. In a New York or London way, in deep midwinter, that could convey a sense of place, couldn't it? Yes, culturally. But what I mean by *sense of place* in the context of this book is horticultural and environmental at heart.

Let me introduce a term I picked up in my late teens and have tried (with varying levels of commitment) to live up to ever since. The term is *deep ecology*. It refers to an understanding of the natural world: our world, your world, the one you live in and somehow derive a living from, no matter how far your daily work may have removed you from the sun and soil. Deep ecology regards humans as one small part of the whole of life. It's an environmental philosophy, not a religion—a way of seeing and approaching life, including your own.

Deep ecology supports thinking holistically, which includes connecting the dots between consumer and consumed. Many of us choose to eat with the seasons, but the industrial economy means we don't have to. Oranges appear in snowstorms, and the same economics are at work in the floral industry, where an Ecuadorian rose might be easier to find (and cost less) than a locally grown dahlia.

Thankfully, the trend of buying local is gradually changing the floral industry, as flower farms catch up to the demand for local product and consumers learn more about the environmental costs of imported flowers. But changing people's perspectives about what constitutes luxury is no easy task. My personal bias toward local flowers isn't solely environmental—it's sensuous, too. I want flowers that smell of more than money, and I want flowers at their peak of perfection. For me, seasonality is key.

Most of the designs in this book could be characterized as *garden style*. That's a term used these days to denote a loose arrangement, not necessarily one composed of garden flowers. But in my case, I grow most of what

I use as a designer. This keeps my work grounded in time and place, and though it poses real restrictions, it also pushes me creatively to make the best of what's on offer. If I can't run to a shop to infill, I'm forced to invent.

As such, you will see many plants included in my designs that aren't available through the floral trade. My garden offers me trees, shrubs, perennials, and biennials. I include them in my designs to open my eyes to different forms of beauty with the hope that others might look at their own gardens in new ways.

If a garden concentrates our experience of nature, an arrangement of flowers and plants does so even more. On a table, in a special corner, above the kitchen sink—we traditionally place flowers where we can enjoy them. We do this to bring the outdoors in. William Morris once said, "The true secret of happiness lies in the taking a genuine interest in all the details of daily life." I say, start with plants.

It's my hope that you will look widely and leave nothing out—not a weed, seedpod, or leaf that speaks to you—and use whatever it is you find provocative, interesting, or beautiful.

# Ecological Style

There is nothing I love more than visiting a garden for the first time, appreciating its unique diversity—its slopes, styles, blooms, stems, and seedheads—and then transposing an image of that garden, and that moment in the garden's life, to the vase.

In a similar way, ecological gardening is place based. It is concerned with habitats, which are living spaces for species botanical, insectivorous, and otherwise; the word *ecology* is derived from the Greek word *oikos* (home).

Like its gardening counterpart, an ecological style of floristry might seek to bring together (loosely, in artistic terms) plants that grow in similar habitats. For example, wild poppies thrive in disturbed ground (hence their sad association with the battlefields of World War I). They also mingle with grasses on roadsides. In this spin on hardscrabble habitat, I've mixed *Papaver rhoeas* with the grasses *Calamagrostis*, *Briza*, and *Pennisetum*; the tiniest *Gypsophila* 'Kermesina', a genus also partial to rocky, dry ground; lavender, another drought-tolerant plant; *Consolida* 'White Cloud'; *Echinacea* 'Green Wizard' (a prairie genus, originally); and some truly wild little tufts of grass.

As my friend Amy Sanderson, who worked in the gardens of Beth Chatto in Essex, England, once said, "For people who know plants . . . using certain species together can mean something or evoke something. Different conditions favor particular plant adaptations and lend an air of aesthetic association."

Such an approach to floristry may, at a deeper level, mean using species as opposed to cultivars and resisting sterile flowers and high-demand ones—flowers that need heat, irrigation, and intense feeding and staking, such as roses, dahlias, and many other flowers produced for their showy blooms alone. This change in focus from marquee flowers to line, twig, and texture can open up a whole range of sustainable options.

Look to various habitats for inspiration: meadows, woodlands, dry Mediterranean landscapes, boggy ground, or roadsides. Beyond thinking just seasonally, ask yourself: What grows with what in the wild?

You needn't be strident; rather, create a loose association between species in the vase. Think in naturalistic gestures, not too dogmatically; evoke.

# Growing Flowers

*The best flower arrangers are the gardeners because they understand how things grow. They don't contrive anything. They just make the flowers speak for themselves.*

—PENNY SNELL

## ON CUTTING GARDENS

Here's what happens when you plant a massive cutting garden: you wade through flowers. Pollen sticks to your pants, seeds stick in your hair, soil travels through socks, and bees are your constant companions.

Most summers, my garden gets gargantuan: the sweet peas sway to seven feet, the cornflowers are easily kissable, and the dahlias become too big to hug. I overorder, overplant, and overindulge every spring, so by midsummer I practically need a machete to cut my way down a path.

I grow on a large urban/suburban lot, so space is at a premium, and thus, soil health is my number one concern. I demand a lot from my plot of earth: growing in zone 7 near the Pacific Ocean means I can plant beds two or three times a year. I regularly bring in manure and feed my soil lime, leaves, compost, organic fertilizer, mycorrhizae, seaweed concoctions, ground bones…You name it. Never above a little juju in the soil department, I've gone through a couple of pails of "glacial rock dust," though I can't even recall what that is.

But I'm getting ahead of myself, because there's a chance you're reading this and thinking: Should I start a cutting garden? How much work is it? Can I sell the flowers from it? Might it pay for itself?

Here we have the issue of economies of scale: yes, you can grow flowers to sell, and you will make money. But it won't be a lot unless you're very clever about how you use those flowers and how many you produce. I'll speak to this point later in the book.

For now, let's tackle the cutting garden as a flowery notion, if not a job. Is it a lot of work? Yes, entirely. It's hard on your back, good for your brain, fantastic for your spirit, and a little tough on your heart. Successfully growing a cutting garden means embracing emotional accountability in the deepest sense of the word: you are responsible for a plant throughout its life. If you abandon one—as an unwatered seedling, as an unpicked bloom—it will respond accordingly.

Some flowers are tough and some climates forgiving, but I bring up this point because it's one of my recurring concerns as a grower. I travel every six weeks for work or pleasure—most often a combination of the two. After a frenzy of gardening, I manage to emotionally let go by getting on a plane, which of course is an eco-negation of sorts, but I think that's half of what I love about traveling—the distance it gives me from daily horticultural demands.

Growing flowers is intense: from seed or cutting or corm—it takes months (and if you count nurturing your soil, a lot longer). Sure, some of the time you had best leave your plants alone and make a cake, throw a party, or actually work at your job, but other times—when you need to weed, pinch back, water, stake, weed again, tie up, and harvest—you must be present. The good news? When we tend a cutting garden, we extend ourselves, both literally and figuratively.

This isn't the book to tell you how to grow a garden, but I hope that despite my honesty it will spur you to find a book that will. Flowers shape my years now. They are both calendar and clock, an all-consuming love I bow to as graciously as I can.

CUTTING YOUR OWN FLOWERS

When cutting your own flowers, a few simple considerations will ensure they last:

1. Flowers picked early in the morning perform best in the vase, followed by flowers picked at night. Why? Transpiration is lowest at these times, so wilting is less likely.

2. Unless you are going for a blousy look, pick your flowers before they are fully mature. They will last longer in the vase.

3. Homegrown flowers are thirsty. See the section on conditioning and remember to check your water levels regularly if you are using a shallow vessel.

4.  You can store flowers in a fridge or cooler for later use. An ideal
    temperature is about 34°F (2°C), which is quite cold, so beware
    of frosting if you block the vents with your bounty.

5.  Keep your tools clean to avoid the spread of disease; wipe snips
    with alcohol and sharpen blades to avoid tearing stems.

6.  Store flowers in a cool, dark place away from ethylene gas, aka
    the ripening hormone. Sources of this gas include fruit, car
    exhaust, smoke, natural gas, and rotting vegetation.

## PRESERVING FLOWERS

"Lovely dead crap" is back, not least of all for its ability to enliven designs
with texture, whimsy, and airiness. Your perspective on dried flowers, or
"everlastings"—from seed heads to preserved leaves to bunches of flowers
hung from beams—may be shaped by personal associations. Remember
those dusty potpourri bowls on toilet tops in the 1980s? Or itchy '70s-style
flower crowns?

Today there's an environmental impetus to move toward dried product. Dried flowers mean no refrigeration and no water in transit. Preserving
the harvest also gives small flower farmers the opportunity to make their
highly perishable products profitable beyond a flower's bloom time, thus
extending their out-of-season income. Dried product, though delicate, can
also be reused.

Some general rules apply to drying flowers:

1.  For best color retention, pick flowers just before they are fully
    mature. Dry them quickly in a dark space; for a bleached look or
    to lighten your plants a shade, keep them in the light.

---

→ A folly of 'Platinum Blonde' dahlias with 'Sun Gold' tomatoes on the vine, *Orlaya*,
*Calendula* 'Snow Princess', *Scabiosa* 'Fama White', *Phlox drummondii* 'Crème Brûlée',
dried hydrangeas, and lunarias. The flowers are supported by a pin frog, with the
tomato clusters wired onto bamboo skewers stuck into the frog.

2. Whatever hangs straight dries straight, so if you'd like to maintain curves or bends, get creative.

3. Ensure your space has some airflow, particularly if you live in a damp climate.

A good introduction to the various methods of preserving flowers can be found in *Julia Clements' Gift Book of Flower Arranging* from 1969. In addition to the Upside-Down Method I've itemized above, Clements describes more advanced techniques, including the Burying Method, which involves using either borax or silica to preserve open-faced flowers like zinnias and marigolds; the Glycerin and Water Method, which explains how woody-stemmed plants and branches of leaves can be preserved; the Pressing Method, useful for ferns and leaves; and Skeletonizing, which was wildly popular in Victorian times and, in my opinion, is wholly in need of a comeback. It involves soaking whole leaves in a vat of water for weeks and then rubbing the flesh off between the veins.

It's both wise and fun to do a little research (other than the trial-and-error variety). Some seedy bits shatter; some blooms, like strawflowers, are best wired; and dried pampas grass, which is in a resurgence at the moment (it was also popular in the Victorian period), is best coated with hairspray to prevent its seeds from wafting.

Drying plants for use in winter is, of course, a very old tradition. I stockpile plants to use in all seasons, predominantly textural creams and browns for use as filler, branches, and seeded plants such as cress and lunaria. As for the indoor displays of dried-flower bouquets, I tend to agree with Gertrude Jekyll's approach, laid out in her 1907 book *Flower Decoration in the House*:

All these dried products of our gardens are welcome ornaments to our rooms in the early winter, though there comes a day somewhere towards the end of February when the evenings are getting longer and the days are full of light, when we find our Iris berries and Chinese Lanterns shrivelled and discoloured, and, thinking of the spring flowers that are soon to come, we burn the whole thing up and are glad to be rid of it.

Drying plants for later use opens up tremendous options for the designer and offers farmers a way to extend their season. Pictured here, freshly picked *Scabiosa* 'Sternkugel', also known as paper moons.

# Foraging and Moving Beyond Flowers

*For how long have we seen, and shall we see,* tame *vases of flowers?*
—CONSTANCE SPRY

## A SPRY STYLE

Constance Spry's name is one many plant lovers will know. David Austin named his first English rose introduction after this floral maven and educator extraordinaire (Spry championed the cultivation of French and old roses in Britain). From 1934 to 1955, Spry published eleven books on floral design and gardening that transformed ideas about style and decoration.

Spry spray-painted leaves white for British decorator Syrie Maugham's iconic all-white drawing room; she used collard greens and seedpods in a shop display on Bond Street in 1926; she counted kale as a fine foliage plant. Spry broke out of the rigid formality of the early part of the century and brought the outside indoors, using wildflowers, native shrubs, and perennials from her garden.

In her book *Flower Decoration*, Spry writes:

> The hedgerows, the vegetable garden, and the orchard are all good sources of supply.... You will want the seed-heads of delphinium, lupin, tritoma, iris, and asphodel, first in their green stage and later when they are sere and brown. You will want the gray-green seeds of seakale flower, and the seeds of sorrel, rhubarb, green artichoke, and onion.

When asked about her penchant for incorporating vegetables in floral design, she once said, "Provided the plant is beautiful, I cannot see why I should not use it for decoration just because it has the added advantage that it can also be eaten."

So in came the marrows and nuts, the foraged and found. Between the wars and beyond, Spry's style proved accessible to all classes and immensely popular.

While I admire the words of Constance Spry, I can't help but see how Gertrude Jekyll's work in the latter part of the nineteenth century paved the way for her success. Jekyll was an English writer and painter who turned

A Thanksgiving centerpiece of pears, grapes, and quinces with fresh hops, peony leaves, hydrangeas, and dahlias. The fruit has been wired or poked onto bamboo skewers and tucked into the chicken-wire frame supporting the flowers. The tufts of immature seeds are from the invasive (in my area) *Clematis vitalba*, known as traveler's joy, given its penchant for relocation. Dispose of such plants responsibly.

Short of filler flowers in June, I harvested branches of the ubiquitous Portuguese laurel, *Prunus lusitanica*, stripped the leaves, and delighted in the froth they offered for my class with Sandy Figel. The blooms looked far sweeter than they smelled, but combined with fragrant philadelphus, sweet peas, stock, and garden roses, this piece by Sandy charmed us both.

to gardening after her eyesight degraded. A fascinating woman of privilege, talent, and taste, she worked with the architect Sir Edwin Lutyens on a number of home and garden projects, including her own home and garden at Munstead Wood.

Jekyll and William Robinson, author of *The English Flower Garden* (1883), have been called "the creators of the herbaceous border." They changed Victorian ideas about flower gardens (semitropicals and contrasting colors having earlier been the rage) and developed what we now think of as the "English garden"—one in which color functions impressionistically. Movement, texture, shape, and color all played to the idea of light in Jekyll's work, and that sensitivity also appeared in her florals.

Compared with Spry's designs, Jekyll's work feels more incendiary, more interesting, and also more grounded. Perhaps it's because I'm a gardener as much as a floral designer, but when I pore over *Flower Decoration in the House*, with its white dahlia and *Clematis flammula* with sea kale and magnolia leaves "in a tall Munstead glass," Jekyll's work feels incredibly modern and her use of annuals, perennials, shrubs, and vines prescient of Spry's later work.

And while Spry, too, had a garden, she also ran a floristry school and a shop in London, where she served a fashionable urban clientele. In the interwar years, during what the British journalist Matthew Dennison has called a period of "flamboyant glamour," Spry socialized and styled with the likes of Cecil Beaton. Her fame eventually reached its pinnacle when she served as florist for the coronation of Queen Elizabeth II in 1953.

As her contemporary and friend Beverley Nichols said of her work, "Constance...has the supreme gift—which really is the core of all art and invention—of seeing things for the first time in a new way, and seeing them whole and seeing them isolated from convention."

There are many things one can learn from Spry's work, but aplomb is one of the most important. Take heart in her words:

> I want to shout out: "Do what you please, follow your own star; be Oriental if you want to be and don't if you don't want to be. Just be natural and gay and lighthearted and pretty and simple and overflowing and general and baroque and bare and austere and stylized and wild and daring and conservative, and learn and learn and learn."

## BY HOOK OR BY CROOK

*What is more irresistible than bringing home objects from the outdoors that were a witness to our enjoyment of nature?*
—GERD VERSCHOOR

Horse chestnut trees, *Aesculus hippocastanum*, bloom in my neighborhood in June, sticky sweet and *bee-u-ti-ful*. One year I'd been eyeing them up, as I'd had a bum year growing *Fritillaria persica* 'Ivory Bells', and the panicles of chestnut blooms reminded me of all I'd missed.

How might I procure some? Number one, the trees are huge, with high crowns. And number two, I feel conflicted about "foraging," as I think the fashion among urbanites is problematic, tempting people to snatch and grab from public places. If we all assume a license to graze, what happens to the resources we share in common?

The phrase "tragedy of the commons" sifted down from my undergrad days, filtering straight through desire and settling on my craving heart. I cursed my environmental studies degree. The gist of the concept is that a shared resource, such as an ocean, a park, or—in my case—a municipal tree, can be subject to exploitation if its users don't exercise individual prudence for the sake of a benefit to all. And that "all" isn't solely human, of course. At the scale of an ecosystem, overuse by any species can lead to collapse. At the scale of a chestnut tree—granted, one with countless blooms—my harvesting would be lessening beauty for my neighbors, impacting bees, and reducing the overall productivity of the tree, which in turn would affect other insects and the birds who eat the insects, as well as the mammals who eat the nuts. You see where holistic thinking can take you (and why it's damned inconvenient in situations of fashion or lust)?

Still, even when I've known better, I've found ways to rationalize foraging. In my early twenties, under headlamp or headlights, I roamed and pillaged, a modern gatherer emboldened by an ethos of eco-self-sufficiency. I lurked around parks at dusk, basket in hand. I harvested nettles in spring and fungi in the fall. Dye plants, healing plants, lichens, moss...no property was safe: college campuses, private forest lands—and, dare I admit, even cemeteries, where I once harvested enough *Ribes sanguineum* blossoms to make a very funky fine wine.

One forager who didn't write in those days but whose judgment I now trust is Pascal Baudar. He advocates taking 10 percent of what's available (and abundant) in a given location. A modern moral guideline, I think. There's nuance to that rule, but what I like about it, and him, is that he knows his sites and ecosystems well. He knows what needs to remain and what can safely, in sustainability terms, be removed. Too few people do.

As I muddled through my chestnut issue, I got to thinking more about forage florists. I do feel that the trend is often positive—a means of showcasing unsung plants and experimenting with new ideas about beauty. One person's weed can be another's treasure. And what excites me most of all about the trend is it gets people outside and identifying plants, which is undoubtedly a benefit to us all.

As *Irish Times* garden writer Fionnuala Fallon says of foraging, "Too many conventional florists treat flowers as fast food, to be ordered as so many stems from Holland or wherever, when they could minimize their imports by utilizing—responsibly—what's in front of their nose."

"Responsibly" is the key: respecting that 10 percent limit. Or in rare-plant situations and fragile ecosystems: 0 percent. Soul death by rare-wildflower picking is guaranteed.

Using invasive species such as traveler's joy, Himalayan blackberries, English ivy, or pokeweed poses other questions: Can you be sure of its proper disposal? In slaughtering the nasties, can you also guarantee they won't spread when dead? If yes, fill a bucket or ten. (If you don't know which plants are invasive in your area, it's easy enough to find out online through local and regional governments. In the United States, the USDA keeps a comprehensive list.)

Like many of us these days, I live in a city with only remnant patches of indigenous vegetation. My chestnut tree (nonnative) was planted as an ornamental tree by the town. In the end, I found a neighbor with one but still wondered, as any urbanite might: If a plant leans over a fence from a privately owned property, could I not snip it when I'm out walking the dog? I've heard you can in California…

Could I not exonerate my future self and spare myself the chitchat with the phrase *by hook or by crook*? It dates from the sixteenth century, first appearing in the scarily titled *Anatomie of Abuses* as: "Either by hooke or crooke, by night or day." It refers to how peasants collected deadwood for fuel on royal lands.

That's *dead*wood, not live. Scrounging by permission. And that's me, doing deals, secateurs in hand.

# Shopping for Materials

## INGREDIENTS MATTER

You can't cook a gorgeous meal without quality ingredients, nor can you design well with subpar flowers. Sure, you can bury your bruised, peel off a petal, and even spin some life into a once-boxed rose by rolling its stem between your hands, but all these tweaks are matters of necessity for most people, not choice.

Similarly, nowhere is it possible to have every flower of your dreams at the same time. So don't feel bad if you can't access quality at first—every designer struggles with scarcity.

Begin by searching for wholesale flowers in your area—either through farms or wholesale operations. See what pops up and if members of the public are permitted to shop. In some major cities flower markets are open to all; in others, decidedly not. Most trade operations open early (around 5 a.m.) and close by noon, so plan ahead. Floral districts and markets often stock floral supplies; when I travel, I always spend an hour poking around to see what's new in the floral trade, be it a vase or flower, before I shop.

The markets in New York, San Francisco, and London all offer floristry supplies and sensational product to the public, so don't miss them, even if it means an early, cold morning and an awkward, laden ride home.

Do note that the scale of purchases at these venues may be more than you bargained for (and that bargaining isn't really welcome). Because professionals shop in these locations, the word *bunch* can mean fifty stems. Don't be afraid to ask for a price if none is posted.

## ON BOTANICAL LATIN

When I was young, I apprenticed to an herbalist in the summer months. She would roll Latin names from her tongue and then pat them into the earth like she was transplanting a delicate seedling: *Rosmarinus*, dew of the sea, the herb of remembrance. To her, plants spoke the poetry of place, and through her stories and sounds of the words, my understanding grew.

When it comes to flowers, it's important to know what you're talking about. Whether growing or buying, try to learn a plant's proper name.

The system used by horticulturalists and knowledgeable floral designers is known as botanical Latin or binomial nomenclature.

The system was developed in the eighteenth century by the Swedish botanist Carl Linnaeus, who organized the influx of plants to Europe into families, giving each living thing two names. The first, which is capitalized, is the genus, the second, the species. Where there is variation or a species has been bred for specific attributes, a third or further names may appear in single quotation marks. For example, the now popular 'Crème Brûlée' phlox would be properly addressed as *Phlox drummondii* 'Crème Brûlée'.

Language can be a portal to increased awareness in the garden. We speak Latin—*clematis, celosia, calendula, crinum*—and we name our world. But there's more to this naming than the representation of a thing: consciousness grows through names. As the Wiccan activist Starhawk once said, "Name a thing and you invoke it." And for me, invocation is linked to the lilt of botanical Latin. Try saying *sisyrinchium* a few times without smiling. Or shape *Rude-BECK-ee-ya* in your mouth. The sound, rhythm, and rhyme of words can lead us to a sensory connection—a deeper connection than reason alone provides—with nature.

When I travel, I know plants will both make me feel like a fumbling foreigner and greet me like old friends. But whether standing in a Dutch bulb market or in a Danish garden, I can call on Latin to converse with local flower fiends. Say, for example, you were on the hunt for corn cockle, a charming wildflower that was abundant in European agricultural fields until the mechanization of farming. The English common name would be precisely that—localized and, in the case of corn cockle, very English at that. Ask an American what corn cockle is and perhaps you'd meet a blank face, but ask for *Agrostemma githago* and you'd be able to find it in a flash.

Latin binomials also reveal flower qualities: *rubra* means "red," *coccineus* means "scarlet," and *luteus* "yellow." The descriptors stick once you get to know the plant; in some cases, the English word isn't too far off the Latin, and in others it's suggestive: *globularis, gigas, reflexus*.

Botanical Latin opens us to new understanding. When I struggle to name the world around me, to trace the family connections of an unknown species or identify the flowers I see in art, I recognize that I will both know and not know. I will be humbled by the territory of botanical understanding that is always, wonderfully, so much wider than the cartography of the self.

# The Paradox of Choice

Why do we suddenly seize up when presented with ten different styles of chrysanthemums? Why do affluent twenty-year-olds thinking of traveling in Europe get tetchy when they have all the freedom in the world?

At the garden center, the flower market, or the boutique, how many of us wander the aisles being drawn hither and yon? We browse and hedge. We need *something*: that's why we carved out time to shop. A decision needs to be made, but what?

That's the trouble with shopping: the paradox of choice.

The psychologist Barry Schwartz coined this phrase to refer to the dissatisfaction we feel when given too much choice. We think we want options, but when faced with too many, we can't easily choose and we second-guess ourselves. Maximizers, people who like to avoid regret, tend to suffer more by seeking "the best," whereas satisficers, people who look for an option that will work, tend to fare better in terms of happiness.

Be a satisficer.

To limit your options when flower shopping, stay firm to your palette. If you're winging it on color, chances are a few flowers will be looking particularly fresh and fantastic, so build your palette out from the gems.

For this autumn arrangement, I wired edible physalises (Cape gooseberries) I found at the market onto dried dogwood branches, pressed them onto a pin frog, and built the arrangement of garden flowers from there.

# Caring for Flowers

## CONDITIONING FLOWERS

The professional term for postharvest care of flowers is *conditioning*. In commercial applications, conditioning involves (usually) a clean cut once the flowers have come in from the field and a resting period in water to which a chemical hydrator and/or a nutrient-based product have been added to encourage flower development. Often an antibacterial agent is used, as well.

The principles of conditioning are important to understand, whether you grow your own flowers or purchase them. If your flowers have been conditioned properly, they won't wilt when you bring them indoors nor be half as thirsty in the vase. However, every type of flower has unique tastes and predilections, so I'll start with some basic principles and get more specific as we go.

Clean water is of the utmost importance. Tepid is better than cold.

When you come home from the shop or in from the garden, strip the lower leaves from stems. Leaves continue to transpire (give off water vapor) after a flower has been cut, so keep only those necessary to your work. In some cases (such as with lilacs), it's best to remove them all.

Different types of flower stems should be treated differently at this stage. The British Florist Association has a handy guide online covering hearty stems, hollow stems, woody ones, milky ones, and so on. Generally speaking, hollow stems (such of those of delphiniums) should be filled with water and plugged using a cotton ball and an elastic. Lupines and amaryllises also have hollow stems and heavy heads, so it's wise to support the flower with a prop. Floral maven Sarah Raven recommends using bamboo cane (I've used barbecue skewers, too) as an insert. Fill the stem with water, place the support inside, trim it to length, and then stuff cotton wool into the hole. Wrap an elastic around the base to hold the whole thing together. Although this might seem tiresome, you'll be thankful you did it.

If you are using woody stems, slit them, score them with an *x*, or smash them with a hammer at their base to allow the stems to absorb more water. Shrubs, blossoming branches, chrysanthemums, and roses all qualify as woody.

The stems of spring bulbs like tulips and hyacinths may have a white portion that doesn't absorb water, so trim this off. Narcissi (daffodils) exude a slimy sap after cutting. Change the water repeatedly before arranging.

Many soft-stemmed plants benefit from a hot-water dip. This method damages the cell walls of stems and allows the cut flower to take up water. Dip about 10 percent of the stem length for about twenty seconds in freshly boiled water, being careful not to steam yourself or the flower. I keep an electric kettle in my studio for opium poppies, *Cerinthe*, and euphorbias. You can try this method with wilted roses, too, adding a teaspoon of sugar to the water they rest in after searing. In a few hours, they may revive.

Another method for quickly treating sappy stems is to burn them. This damages the stem so it can absorb water and also seals it off, preventing wilting. If I have a small number of Icelandic poppies, I'll simply sear the stems with a barbecue lighter. (Flower farmers use propane blowtorches.) Just run the flame along the lower portion of the stem until it goes semi-transparent and the sap bubbles and burns a bit at the cut end of the stem.

Foliage can be revived just as you might lettuce for a salad. Place the leaves in a cool bath, then shake off excess water and store them at a low temperature to perk.

After whatever special treatment you've doled out (the requirements of each type of flower can be a bit intimidating, but you learn them over time), leave your flowers to rest in deep water, in a cool place away from direct sunlight. Try to leave them for a few hours or overnight before arranging.

Carefully top up your vessel with water after arranging; use a small watering can for fitting in between stems.

Remember to keep your arrangement away from sun and heat.

→ Workshop materials arranged with Rachael Scott and Sarah Statham

## KEEPING FLOWERS FRESH

Every living thing carries a microbiome, flowers included. In vase water, bacteria propagate, feeding off their primary food source—the cut ends of stems. The stems degrade eventually (giving old vase water that special swampy stench), but before that point the bacteria clog your plant's stem capillaries, preventing them from taking up water and shortening the vase life of your flowers. (This is why freshly cutting stems is often recommended to prolong the life of flowers.)

I religiously change water daily and advise my customers to do the same. (If the water can't be poured out easily, just run fresh water into the flowers to flush.) Additives can also help. Sarah Raven advises, "What cut flowers need is a balance of sugars that can be utilized for metabolism, a substance to raise the acidity of the water and an antibacterial agent. Commercial sachets of cut-flower food contain agents for all three." If you don't have "flower powder" or if you eschew plastic packages or those mysterious substances known as "agents," you can, as Raven suggests, improvise with a teaspoon of sugar and a couple drops of bleach. I've also heard vodka can work to retard the growth of bacteria.

If I seem reluctant to advocate specific products or potions, it's because each type of flower has its own response to various substances (astilbes, aye to alcohol; asclepias, yea to sugar), and the level of detail involved in itemizing who loves what could crush your enthusiasm. If, however, you're one of those conscientious people who like to be armed with all the facts, seek out "Conditioning Flowers," a wonderful flower-by-flower online list of management and care compiled by the garden club of Brookfield, Connecticut. Sarah Raven also offers detailed advice in her now-classic 1996 book *The Cutting Garden*. I highly recommend it.

Flowers alter as they age. From bud break to bloom to fully mature and, finally, fading, a flower changes in form and color over time. The 'Honey Dijon' rose at center is a great example of how varied a flower might appear, depending on its age. With buds tinged in orange, the flower opens a deep mustard, then softens to maize before finally dropping buff-brown petals.

## TENDER PLANTS USEFUL FOR ARRANGING

Houseplants, tropicals, and semitropicals are often long-lasting, but be sure to check their conditioning requirements when cutting your own.

**Abutilon:** Beautiful pendulous flowers and fresh green leaves make this a great choice to sit in a bright window indoors or as a pot-grown plant that summers outdoors. Strip the leaves and crush or sear the stems in hot water before arranging.

**Anthurium:** Cut the stems under water. These glossy tropicals last well.

**Begonia:** Foliage fiends, rejoice; it is possible to use begonias. Float leaves in a water bath to condition; make sure their short stems are submerged in your arrangement. If you are using whole stems (such as those of the hardy *Begonia grandis*), you may get lucky and the stems might take root.

**Bougainvillea:** The Garden Club of Brookfield, Connecticut, advises: "Remove foliage and thorns. Split stems, dip in boiling water for a few seconds, and submerge the spray in cold water for several hours. Stand in deep water for one hour or more to drip dry. Recut stems under water if shortening them for an arrangement. Spray regularly with a fine mist of cool water."

**Caladium:** The leaves of these stunning plants need a hot-water dip and a deep soak in cool water before arranging.

**Coleus:** These wilt quickly without a brief dip of the stem in hot water and resting time in cool water.

**Croton:** The variegated leaves of croton plants (*Codiaeum variegatum*) are sold commercially, but you can harvest your own. Be careful of the sap if you're allergic to euphorbias, and let it bleed out in cool water before arranging.

**Ferns:** A good rule of thumb with ferns (whether grown in the garden or house) is to wait until they are sexually mature to use them—in other words, once the spores are brown. As they are delicate, hydrate them in a water bath before arranging.

**Fuchsia:** Give these a boiling-water dip before a long drink of cool water.

**Maidenhair Fern:** Hot-water dip as much of the tough stem as possible, being careful not to steam the leaves. Leave the ferns in the water until it cools, then tie a plastic bag overtop. Let sit for at least a day in a cool spot before arranging.

**Pelargonium:** Half-hardy and easily grown in terra-cotta pots on a balcony in summer and brought indoors in winter, scented geraniums are particularly useful in floral design, offering both fragrance and long-lasting leafy stems.

**Philodendron:** 'Elephant Ear' leaves can last out of water for a week, once conditioned.

**Poinsettia:** Poinsettias are euphorbias, which means they exude a sticky, white sap (some people are allergic to this plant family). To condition these plants, cut the stems and rinse the sap off, then slice a line up the stem. Dip the stem in boiling water for twenty seconds, then leave them to rest in cool water for a few hours. If you treat them this way, and if your arrangement is in a cool room, you can expect almost a week of glamour from their showy bracts.

**Water Lilies:** Water lilies continue to open and close once cut, following a schedule of either night blooming or day blooming, depending on the variety. I've read that dripping wax between the petals can force the flower to stay open; another method is to deeply chill them then warm them up, which will give you a few hours of bloom time. I've allowed them to follow their natural cycle and found they last well for about four days. They benefit from sugar in their water.

# Ripe and Ready

We are talking about flowers, so sexual innuendo is entirely apt. Flowers are the reproductive structures of higher plants. They serve a purpose—to attract pollinators, with the singular goal of making more of their kind. We might think of them as beauties alone, demure in countenance, or sterile showstoppers, bred into submission, but don't underestimate nature, no matter how manipulated by human hands; most flowers are, thankfully, nothing short of wanton libido made manifest.

And I like the experienced ones best.

Do you make banana bread from young fruit? Eat a hard peach? Never. If you're like me, you nibble that bit of orange just around the moldy spot because it's the orangiest, the best. My friend, the chef Mara Jernigan, once recited this truism: *C'est le vieux légume que fait le bon potage* (It is the old vegetable that makes the good soup). I agree.

Blousy and blown flowers are often the most evocative. They've been open to the world for a while, and that serves me as a designer as well as the planet. I may moan about poppies losing their pollen to bees before I pluck them, but really, isn't that the point of my work—and the flowers'? To ensure more life, not less—to share what I've grown with both people and the insects who ensure me seed?

I'll take my tulips hanging full and heavy, thank you, relaxed in postcoital repose.

No one expects the arugula served at dinner to last a week. And a fresh cob of corn's sweetness, even less. This may not help when you're grabbing a few bunches at the grocery store, but perhaps wait a few days to use your flowers, so they have a chance to relax.

Life is short and epic and tragic and joyful, so give me a day or two of perfection over a week of mediocrity. Smudge me with pollen right between my eyes.

---

→ This selection of deep and light pinks from Rose Story Farm in Carpinteria, California, includes (clockwise from upper left): 'Climbing Shot Silk', with a yellow center; 'Tiffany', at top; and 'Christopher Marlowe', with a touch of ruffled yellow. The pale pink rose below 'Christopher Marlowe' with the peachy center is 'Madame Paule Massad', and at bottom right is 'Jubilee Celebration'. The pale pink rose at the base of the arrangement is 'D. A. Kathryn Morley', with 'Princess Alexandra of Kent' to her left.

# PART TWO

# GEARING UP

# A (Flower) Room of One's Own

Years ago, I was dead set on being tidier and saving time and so reasoned that converting my office into a scullery/mud room/flower room was a perfect way to cover my muddy tracks.

Once two walls would be taken down, I'd have a clear path to a bathroom from outdoors, a boot/coat storage area, and a dog zone, wipeable after every shake. I could wear my boots inside, and when I harvested flowers or vegetables, there would be a compost bin and sink to process them right there.

Oh, how that scullery sang to me. It intoned old England with shelves for vases and an indoor/outdoor cupboard, ratproofed to store perishables without refrigeration. My scullery shunned suburban conveniences for a more grounded life. And flowers were at the center of it.

Constance Spry once described the attributes of a fine flower room:

> One wants cupboards for vases, deep pails for cut flowers—the variety sold to florists are best, as they are deeper and narrower than the ordinary kind—mops for cleaning, silver sand and a bottle of Milton for removing stains from the inside of vases. A teak sink is an insurance against breakage but a large papier-mâché bowl will serve, and if the tap is protected with a piece of rubber tubing, one is less likely to chip the vases.

So I had an architect come over to measure and plot. She made drawings. And for the hundred thousand dollars she quoted, I reasoned that I could occasionally pee outside.

Even after having set up an unheated floral studio in my garage, I still yearn for a space that blends the outside and in. I do have great worktables that I designed, with wrapped steel tops at almost Julia Child heights, which helps my posture while I work. These are on wheels with locking casters, allowing me to change the layout of the space. The floor is concrete—not glamorous but always cool. A deep sink means I can wash large containers and racks mean I can dry them, while shelves for vases free up counter space.

The rafters have been used to cure garlic and hold dried flowers and seed heads. The studio is bright because of a skylight, so dried flowers

bleach out, and the air is damp, so they occasionally mildew, but I have managed to run my business from said studio/garage for a few years. I've built wreaths in winter wearing fingerless gloves and in summer positioned long installation pieces across the floor.

I know people who have built floral businesses from their kitchen tables and others who have barns, coolers, hoop houses, shops, workrooms, and offices. I'm sure there's an economy of scale at play, but the point is: start where you are.

# Vessels

**TO HAVE AND TO HOLD**

I typed: "I've never been married, so I don't own china." Then I leaned back, appalled.

I read the sentence again, trying to admire its declarative power, its nicely placed comma, but my words were loaded with more feminine angst than a copy of *Mrs. Beeton's Book of Household Management*, circa 1861. Wherefore such woe?

In my mind, in my late thirties, marriage equaled china. Where had I come up with such an association? Even if I'd been married when I was younger, I wouldn't have registered for china. How, for a middle-aged woman who called herself a feminist, had it come to that?

From medieval times until the early twentieth century, women of European descent collected keepsakes and household items in preparation for their marriage. Clothing, mementos, needlework, and china were kept in a trunk known as a hope chest. This chest constituted a part of a woman's dowry—historically, the mark of a woman's worth; in modern times the hope chest came to act more as a bridge between domestic worlds, a quaint way to carry things from the past into one's future. This explains my marital association, but there's more to unpack from the idea of a hope chest. What do we carry from our past? And what does that stuff say about who we are now?

There's a brilliant passage in *The Things They Carried* by Tim O'Brien in which the author lists the objects a squadron of American soldiers carry through Vietnam. Each item reveals something about the character who carried it, and the more specific the item is, the more we see the humanity of the man. One carries canned peaches. Another, a diary. And another, hotel-size bars of soap. From each detail we build a personality—tastes, comforts, and affections—and, by extension, the hopes that shape a life.

---

← An old silver rose bowl playing host to a spring garden of maple tree blossoms, fritillarias, *Erythronium* 'Pagoda', and tulips

Vases and vessels similarly tell stories. They express aesthetic understanding, political sensibilities, class, utility, and often a history independent of us, whether through a patina, a chip, or the material and style of the vessel itself.

As such, the relationship between vessels and flowers is a long and intimate one.

## ON VESSELS

A vessel is a form. Before you place the first flower in a bowl, vase, urn, or tazza, you are faced with an artistic decision: How can I make the content speak to the form and vice versa?

Let's take a look at some styles of vessels, in the hope that their backstories might enliven your designs:

**Amphora:** Amphorae were used to transport oil and grain, so their neck is narrow, the body bulbous, and the base tapered. The word comes from Greek *amphi* (on both sides) and *phero* (to carry). Amphorae usually have handles affixed near the neck.

**Baluster Vase:** Fashionable in Europe during the seventeenth century, a baluster vase is shaped like an urn; its lid has holes for the placement of individual flowers.

**Basket:** Low woven baskets were among the first vessels used by humans for the display of flowers. In ancient China, Roman times, the Egyptian period, the medieval period, and later in the Dutch Golden Age, baskets served as collection vessels and also as containers for display. Openwork porcelain and silver baskets became popular in the eighteenth century. While today we have plastic inserts for baskets meant for horticultural purposes, you can also improvise with low glass or metal baking dishes. Constance Spry, a fan of adorning nooks and walls, once used a bicycle basket filled with jam jars for a mounted display.

**Bud Vase:** Intended to showcase a single bloom, bud vases can also be grouped to create a vignette.

This English Fulham Pottery fan vase has interior supports for stems, pictured here with *Hesperis* seed heads, poppies, *Ammi*, and *Colutea arborescens*.

**Bulb Pot:** A container with some form of collar to hold a bulb just above the water for forcing.

**Cache Pot:** From the French *cacher* (to hide) comes the name of this vessel, designed to hold a flowerpot.

**Compote/Comport/Tazza:** A compote is technically a dessert dish that is elevated by a stem, and a comport is similar but shallower. A tazza (from the Italian) may be an elevated glass cup but is most often a delicate, wide, shallow dish elevated on a stem; like compotes and comports, it is supported by a foot.

**Cornucopia:** From the Latin *cornu copiae* (horn of plenty), a cornucopia is shaped like a goat's horn. From the time of the ancient Greeks, it has symbolized abundance. Originally made of basketry, cornucopias today can be found in a variety of materials, from plastic to porcelain.

**Cuvette:** Used for both flowers and bulbs, cuvettes were sometimes divided into compartments and some had holes for stems. Low and often placed in groups, they were made of porcelain in the eighteenth century.

**Cuvette Mahon:** A more or less rectangular, low French vessel with four scrolled feet, originally made of porcelain in the eighteenth century.

**Delftware:** Delft is a town in the Netherlands that began specializing in the production of blue-and-white pottery in the seventeenth century, after Dutch traders returned from China with porcelain. *Kast-stel* sets consisting of lidded storage jars are still produced today, as is a wide range of Delftware.

**Ewer:** A pitcher or jug.

**Fan Vase:** Fan vases have taken many forms over the centuries, some resembling a fingered glove (known as a quintal horn), with later ones known as "five-fingered posy holders." Some fan vases resemble actual fans, while others look somewhat like giant clamshells, as is the case with pieces designed by Constance Spry in the 1930s and '40s.

**Flower Brick/Bough Pot:** Flower bricks and bough pots are similar; both were traditionally made of porcelain and contained holes for cut flowers. Bough pots were often used in fireplaces in summer.

**Flower Ring:** A low trough for the display of petite blooms, popular in the 1920s and '30s.

**Footed Bowl:** Many varieties of footed bowls exist; they are tremendously useful for opulent centerpieces, given their wide mouth and elevated design.

**Ginger Jar:** A high-shouldered porcelain vessel originally used to transport spices. Ginger jar lids are usually domed. They have been used as decorative items for hundreds of years but also make fine vessels for flowers, despite their relatively narrow openings.

**Jardiniere:** A low, open vessel traditionally used as a flowerpot holder or planter.

**Krater:** An open, wide, footed vessel with handles, used by the Etruscans for the mixing of wine and water. Many styles are still in evidence today (which we might call urns): the calyx, with small handles set low on the vessel; the bell krater, with handles near the rim; the column krater, with handles bridging the bulbous body and the rim; and the volute krater, often with scroll-like handles set above the lip of the vessel. The neoclassical period in Europe revitalized a number of these designs.

**Mantel Vase:** Oblong mantel vases can be used on windowsills and have been produced for centuries. Constance Spry commissioned a line of mantel vases that are (forgive me) oddly reminiscent of the female reproductive organs, with two fallopian-style tubes looping back to a uterine-shaped base. These were produced by Fulham Pottery from the 1930s to the '50s.

**March Stand:** In the Victorian period, march stands adorned dining tables. These consisted of a series of cone-shaped flower holders or low dishes set in tiers, which allowed diners to see across the table. Earlier, silver epergnes were used on dining tables to hold fruit, sweets, and flowers. Stands would

A Chinese celadon bowl in the drawing room of Cambo House near St Andrews, Scotland, likely Ming dynasty (dating from between the late fourteenth and mid-seventeenth centuries), holds a collection of plants from the garden and local flower farmers. The bright-orange flowers are *Bulbine frutescens*; the orange and red flowers are from the tender vine *Ipomoea lobata*. The purples here include xeranthemums, nepetas, and *Salvia leucantha*. The two ginger jars in the background play well with the pastel tones of the arrangement.

continue to be popular into the Edwardian period and beyond, reaching ever greater heights until finally they were abandoned and whole palms and other trees emerged from the tables built around them.

**Meiping Vase:** The Chinese word *mei* may refer to prunus (flowering plum), and the word *ping* to a vessel or vase. Meiping vases are tall and high-shouldered, with a small mouth and tapered base. This style originated in the Song dynasty (960–1279) and became a standard form in the Ming (1368–1644).

**Moon Flask or Pilgrim's Flask:** Known as *bianhu* in Chinese, which translates to "flattened vase," this receptacle has its origin in the leather vessels carried by Central Asian nomads. According to the art historian Audrey Wang, "the shape was commonly used in fifth- and sixth-century pottery, and the trend was revived in porcelain in the Ming and Qing dynasties with decorations in blue and white."

**Posy Vase:** A porcelain vessel with holes set within it to support stems.

**Rose Bowl:** A glass or silver bowl with a metal grid cover.

**Transferware:** English porcelain printed with intricate scenes, particularly popular in North America in the nineteenth century.

**Trumpet Vase:** Popular in the Victorian period, trumpet vases were used singly and also in branched forms for a variety of cut flowers and ferns.

**Tulipiere/Flower Pyramid:** A seventeenth-century invention for the growing of bulbs, often consisting of stackable containers that, when assembled, are reminiscent of a pagoda. Tulipieres have narrow-necked spouts to support the stems of individual flowers.

**Tureen:** A covered serving dish for hot foods. Styles have varied since the seventeenth century—from ornate silver and porcelain pieces to ceramic cabbages and rabbit-shaped vessels.

**Urn:** A rounded vessel with a footed pedestal. Urns have assumed many forms throughout history; today we tend to think of the classical Greek variety, with either stylized or practical handles on either side. Lidded funerary urns have been used for millennia throughout the world for cremated remains.

**Wall Pocket:** From the nineteenth century onward, a number of devices have been manufactured for the display of flowers on walls. Constance Spry was a big fan of wall pockets and argued for their practicality at parties, where guests might enjoy flowers without running into them.

## VESSEL MATERIALS

The material of a vessel plays a key role in determining an arrangement's style. For example, pewter and iron convey solidity, while brass strikes a higher note. Ceramics vary dramatically by type and glaze, and porcelain often bears designs and color. Here are some common materials floral designers use:

**Alabaster and Marble:** Alabaster is a relatively soft sedimentary rock that can be easily carved, whereas marble is metamorphic and harder. Both have been used throughout the world for millennia to make sculptures, decorative panels, urns, and vessels. Alabaster is translucent, and thin pieces of alabaster were used in medieval churches for windowpanes. Don't clean marble or alabaster with acidic substances or bleach; use paint thinner, aka white spirit.

**Basketry:** Plants in plants—what could be better? If baskets held water! The art of basketry is an ancient one. Throughout history, branches have been bent, grasses woven, and needles bound to create beautiful objects that deserve more consideration.

**Blown Glass:** Glassblowing dates from around 50 BCE. Modern pieces in blown glass are often so decorative they don't need flowers.

**Bone China:** Real bone china, like fine porcelain and lead crystal, sings. Bone china is, in fact, made from bones. Not *entirely* of bones, but about 40 percent bone ash in finer pieces. Think cremated cows. Think nose-to-tail dining—then imagine a man standing on a teacup, performing a stunt sales reps once used to illustrate bone china's strength.

**Brass:** An age-old alloy of copper and zinc. The archaeological record shows brass has been in production since the first millennium BCE. Brass is a favorite of mine for its low-luster shine and low price point. Look for vintage pieces from India, Morocco, and the Middle East.

**Bronze:** A material composed mainly of copper, with the addition of tin or other metals. Historically in Chinese culture, bronze vases were chosen for winter and spring arrangements.

**Cast Iron:** Most of the cast-iron urns we associate with flowers and gardens today come from the Victorian period, when outdoor arrangements were in vogue. Modeled on classical forms and occasionally ornate, they are terrifically heavy, which is a blessing for large floral pieces but too unwieldy for most designers. Smaller campana (from the Spanish, meaning "bell-like") shapes or low, open tazza shapes are the easiest to wrangle. Do note that iron rusts easily; in the presence of a lead-based pin frog or zinc-coated steel chicken wire, electrochemical corrosion advances at an even faster rate.

**Ceramic:** A catchall word for a variety of clay-based products that might include earthenware, terra-cotta, porcelain, bone china, and pottery.

**China:** China might be thought of as imitation porcelain; it can be referred to as *china*, *fine china*, or *bone china*.

**Concrete:** A blend of cement (interestingly, the world's most-used resource, next to water), sand, and aggregate. Stonelike and recyclable, concrete/cement is an inexpensive choice offering heft and a neutral tone.

**Copper:** Warm in color and flexible, this metal has a long history of use for kitchen and pantry ware, but a number of vessel styles can be repurposed for floristry. The seams of old copper vessels don't always hold water, hence its association with dried-flower ensembles.

**Depression Glass:** Colored, molded, and printed with patterns, Depression glass takes its name from the Great Depression in the United States, when it was first produced. While once inexpensive and given away as a marketing incentive for other products, it's now a collector's item.

**Earthenware:** An early form of pottery, fired at a low heat, earthenware, like terra-cotta, is porous. Glazed versions can hold water and offer a wonderful rustic sensibility, as evidenced by Japanese raku ware.

**Frosted Glass:** Glass that has been treated with caustic acid to soften its appearance and diffuse light

**Glass:** Glass has been in production since 3500 BCE. I rarely use clear glass, with the exception of bud vases, as I have too much going on underwater—revealing it would be like showing off my Spanx. That said, you can line a glass vase with large leaves to conceal stems and infrastructure. Glass takes many forms, listed as separate entries below.

**Gold:** Having never designed in pure gold, I can't rightly speak to this material, but if you're lucky enough to have done so, send me a picture.

**Lead Glass/Crystal:** Crystal is a form of glass to which oxides have been added. Originally, lead oxide was used in crystal glassware; modern versions don't contain it (due to health concerns about drinking from leaded crystal), though high-quality vases still do. Lead glass sings when tapped, thanks to the oscillation of the lead crystals. Contemporary crystal without lead is lighter and refracts less light.

**Lucite/Plexiglas/Acrylic:** Developed in the 1930s, these petrochemical compounds can be cut into stark, clean lines or molded into curved, abstract shapes. They are highly durable, UV-resistant, and environmentally persistent; look for pieces in thrift shops.

**Mercury Glass:** Once known as poor man's silver, inexpensive mercury glass today is faked with metallic paint (and therefore rubs off) but originally was made of double-walled glass with a thin layer of silvering compound held between the layers. Popular for wedding florals, the modern versions work well if you don't scrub too hard when cleaning.

**Milk Glass:** Originally produced in Italy in the sixteenth century, milk glass became popular at the end of the nineteenth century. It is conventionally milky white, though it also can be colored; throughout its history, the same ingredients that have been used in ceramic glazes have been added to its production.

**Pewter:** Gray and wonderfully matte, pewter is made predominantly from tin. I associate pewter with the Tudor period in England, seventeenth-century Dutch still life painting, and the early American colonial period, though that was near the material's decline for everyday use. It has been the primary metal used domestically since Roman times. Modern pewter is lead-free and made from tin, copper, and antimony. Unlike silver, it tarnishes very slowly.

**Plaster:** Used since prehistoric times for the casting of molds and in the decorative arts, plaster needs to be sealed before it will hold water.

**Porcelain:** Porcelain is made from clay, kaolin clay, and other mineral additives. The fineness of the clay permits it to be shaped into intricate details. Porcelain is the only form of ceramic that transmits light. It was developed in China during the Han dynasty (206 BCE–220 CE). Specific vase shapes were developed in China to serve individual flower types and branches.

**Pottery:** A form of ceramic in which clay is hand thrown or sculpted and fired. Pottery is often glazed and then refired, making most modern pottery vessels watertight.

**Silver:** Polished silver reflects light and has a cool, bright shine that few metals can match. Sterling silver is an alloy of copper and silver and tarnishes more quickly than pure silver. Use caution when using chicken wire (even the plastic-coated kind) in silver vessels—corrosion happens fast.

**Slip-Cast Ceramics:** Mass-produced using molds, as opposed to thrown on a wheel, slip-cast pottery forms most of modern porcelain production, as intricate shapes—everything from toilets to teapots to tureens—can be efficiently produced.

**Stoneware:** Stoneware has had minerals added to the clay, so it is stronger than earthenware. Fired at higher temperatures, it is not porous and can hold water unglazed, though it often is glazed on the interior.

**Terra-Cotta:** Wonderfully versatile and warm in color from the iron content of the clay, terra-cotta doesn't hold water unless treated with a sealer.

**Zinc:** Through galvanization, zinc can be used to protect other metals from rusting. Developed at an industrial scale in the 1830s, the process has provided us with long-lasting watering cans, planters, and flower buckets.

# On Being an Amateur

*When you are learning how to do something, you do not have to
worry about whether or not you are good at it. But when you have done
something, have learned how to do it, you are not safe any more.
Being an expert opens you up to judgement.*
—HELEN MACDONALD

Expertise can limit a person. While a seasoned florist may know what lives or dies and what goes with what, inexperience and curiosity can lead to innovation.

Radiohead's front man, Thom Yorke, once named his greatest strength: "That I don't know what I'm doing."

Neither did I in using unconditioned *Cobaea* vines for this arrangement of September dahlias and asters, but it worked for a bit.

The social scientist Francesca Gino studies rebels and nonconformists as a part of her work at the Harvard Business School. Her research reveals that knowing less can often mean knowing more—in terms of creative problem solving. And rule breakers are often the most creative of all.

Confidence, Gino says, comes from stepping outside norms and succeeding. If you are an amateur, you naturally break rules when you try to solve problems because you don't know better: no palette prescriptives, no recipes—nothing except the plants before you.

I so often see the wonder of naivete in workshops where the complete novice soars. I wish I could go back to *not* knowing some days.

Be grateful for your freedom. Be curious. See what might work and notice what doesn't. Make your own rules.

# Mechanics

## FAREWELL FLORAL FOAM

Once upon a time, in a place of limited insight and great innovation, people made foam from petroleum and stuck plants in it. I'm talking about floral foam, of course, brand-named Oasis: that green stuff that soaks up water and holds stems in place. It's still used today, sadly. Floral foam is plastic (an old form of phenol-formaldehyde resin), and no amount of greenwashing can convince me it isn't harmful to the environment. Floral foam, when disposed of in water (or on land) doesn't fully break down, and tiny particles of plastic persist for decades. This is most distressing in marine and freshwater environments, where microplastics choke off life.

I'm not even mentioning the impact floral foam has on human health, because to me planetary health trumps individualism. Suffice it to say, floral foam is to contemporary floristry what asbestos is to home building—dated and dangerous.

Modern styles have become more relaxed, which raises the question: Which came first—the romance of looser lines or the rebellion against foam's forms?

Floral foam holds even tiny stems upright, can be cut into shapes, and holds flowers at obtuse angles. So how do we simulate that look? We dig back into the preplastic period to excavate some of the old tools of the trade—namely, pin frogs, chicken wire, and props borrowed from nature. Constance Spry designed vases with internal supports and opted for pin frogs over glass frogs, praising them: "For shallow bowls there is a new flower support, new at least to me, which I think admirable. Made of heavy lead, it is studded thickly with sharp points, like a coarse metal brush. These hold flowers in place and at the same time pierce the ends of the stems so that water is easily absorbed." At the turn of the twentieth century, Gertrude Jekyll had recommended using pea sticks (twiggy supports from a wood

---

→ Elm and ninebark branches with *Narcissus* 'Yellow Cheerfulness', 'Apricot Whirl', 'White Lion', and 'Petit Four'; *Fritillaria ulva vulpis*; *Erysimum* 'Sunset Primrose'; and *Akebia*.

like hazel), commenting, "The neutral colour of the bark makes the support almost invisible." Today, florists innovate with branches available in their region, zip-tie trumpet vases onto standing wood, design arbors that might hold buckets, and achieve height in clever ways, inventing alternatives and finding creative solutions, foam-free.

TOOLS OF THE TRADE

Tools for floral design are easily found online and at flower markets and garden centers. Few items are expensive, but there are varying degrees of quality. Make snips your primary investment.

**Anchors:** These vary from pin frogs to glass stem holders to metal cage frogs.

**Bamboo Skewers and Canes:** Used to support sappy and weak stems or to provide more height.

**Chicken Wire:** Also known as poultry netting or wire netting, chicken wire comes in rolls and may be coated in plastic. I use (and reuse, after running it through the dishwasher) the plastic-coated variety, as I find it gentler on vases and easier to slide stems through. Copper netting is very pliable and has smaller holes, making it a great choice for odd-shaped vessels.

**Elastic Bands:** I use a number of elastics when making bouquets, offering me the flexibility to stick in more stems before taping the whole project with floral stem wrap.

**Floral Putty:** Floral putty, also called clay, will hold your anchors in place underwater.

**Floral Stem Wrap:** This tape has a crepe-paper appearance but gets tacky when stretched.

**Floral Wire:** Wire comes in a variety of gauges and styles for uses ranging from wreath work to wiring individual flowers. Invest in a pair of wire cutters so you're not tempted to ruin your snips cutting wire.

**Gloves:** Leather for roses, nitrile for other tasks. I rarely design in gloves but process most flowers with them on; with gloves on, you can easily slide a hand down a stem to strip off leaves.

**Mirror:** Incredibly useful for bridal bouquets, a mirror allows you to view your work as it will be seen.

**Snips:** I use heavy bypass pruners for branches, but the clippers I keep in my pocket are lightweight needle-nose snips with a spring-loaded handle. These tend to poke a hole in even jeans pockets over time, so try to use a tool belt.

**Thorn Stripper:** A handy device to save yourself from puncture wounds.

**Tool Belt:** I have a leather belt, which means I don't lose my tools and damage my clothes. I use it for gardening as well as designing, as it's large enough to carry a trowel, plant tags, wire, and snips.

**Turntable/Lazy Susan:** Useful for viewing your work from a number of angles.

**Waterproof Floral Tape:** I tape down a loose ball of chicken wire in a vessel by making a cross with thin, waterproof floral tape across the opening of my vessel. A puttied pin frog with a cage of wire in place overtop provides the necessary infrastructure to achieve interesting angles and shapes with stems. Frog, then wire, then tape, then water.

**Zip ties:** Handy if you can't find wire, these plastic fasteners are useful for installation work.

# Torque

An ode to spring, this arrangement uses the branches of flowering plum to create a three-sided stage for showier blooms.

Branches can be hard to direct. Heavy, long, and ideally curving, they tend to lean and twist, so I press them onto a pin frog, or *kenzan* (as it is known in ikebana, the ancient Japanese method of flower arranging). In a light, shallow vessel, a quality pin frog adds valuable weight. Tack it in place with floral adhesive clay.

I almost always tape chicken wire over a *kenzan* when working with branches (unless the branches are too large and won't fit through the wire holes, in which case a grid of floral tape across the opening of the vessel can help hold things in place). With shallow vessels, it's vitally important to balance the whole arrangement.

A little physics lesson is in order here because it's fun to have the right language to describe why something works (or, in the case of a spilled shallow dish of branches, why it didn't). The *kenzan*/wire/vessel combo functions as a pivot point around which the entire arrangement rotates. I wanted it to be both literally and figuratively the center of mass for this arrangement.

The farther away we place something from the pivot point (and the heavier it is), the greater the force working against that point, which means that eventually your pin frog will unstick and the whole shebang will flip over. *Torque* is the technical term for this phenomenon, and it's calculated by how much force acts on your pin frog/wire/vessel, causing that object to rotate, as well as by the number of expletives you utter while working. When we go low with heavy outlying fruit or branches, we increase force and the potential for torque, beauty, and disaster.

I have some heavy galvanized shackles from a marine-supply store I use if I need to offset torque; I just drop them into the vessel or attach them to the base of a branch. Interestingly, in biomechanics the term *moment* is similar to torque—it means force times the distance to your axis of rotation. In physics, these branches might be called *moment arms*. Rather apt.

PART THREE

# THINKING
# ABOUT
# COLOR

# Painting with Flowers

I once tried to paint the feeling I had when my husband first kissed me. In an acrylics class, I ripped off a four-foot piece of canvas and hung it lengthwise on the easel. I started painting in bright turquoise and brilliant greens, then used jet black India ink to outline my uncle's pool in Key West where we kissed and the palms surrounding it. The ink dripped down the length of the canvas, making the image look steamy but sinister, so I dipped my brush in orange and magenta to fill the spaces with light. I spent the remainder of the class trying to get that rosy orange right, to make it glow like the shade of sunrise or the thin line of color your teeth cut between the skin and flesh of a plum.

I never finished that painting.

Fast-forward eleven years, and I was planning my wedding to that same man, which meant I had to pick colors. I realized that although color had always called to me, I didn't fully understand it.

I signed myself up for a color theory class at the local art college. It remains, to this day, one of the most difficult classes of my life (on par with linguistics). Why? Because I didn't know how to see or name what I saw. I had no language, visual or verbal, for color.

Like the common names of plants, flower colors shift with geography. Indoors, we may be viewing flowers in artificial light, which changes how we see them. In the garden, flower color changes over the course of the day. As the great gardener Rosemary Verey once said:

> Colors change; in the morning light, red shines out bright and clear and the blues merge into their surroundings, melting into the greens; but by evening the reds lose their piquancy, embracing a quieter tone.... Yellow flowers remain bright, and white ones become luminous, shining like ghostly figures against a darkening green background.

Understanding where, when, and how flowers will be used is a wise way to approach color. But before you even head outside with your snips or down to the market for blooms, let's define what we are really talking about when we talk about color.

Most people can see about 17,000 different colors, but learning to see color as a designer takes work. Notice how the hues on the right advance out from the picture, looming larger, while the cool blues and purples recede. (There's a slight trick of light here as well, given that the light source—a window—is at the right.) In this composition the shape of the arrangement is roughly symmetrical while the colors are obviously not. Outlandish designs often benefit from a point of stability—in this case, form remains constant while the rainbow arches over the work.

# Color and Perception

Occasionally, I make myself a little batty trying to understand why colors work together. I can see that they do and know that they please me or a client, but I often want to decode my intuition after the fact.

After making this little ensemble, I read about Johann Wolfgang von Goethe's color theories and how his ideas shaped the Impressionists' use of color. Next thing I knew, I was deep into nineteenth-century Paris, its streets lined with flower shops and its gardeners working to find the next fashionable flower. And fashionable Paris was: all that energy put into beauty and adornment also meant research into fabric dyes and color.

Enter Michel Eugène Chevreul, who began his career at the Jardin des Plantes in Paris but was hired as a chemist by the Gobelins tapestry company in 1839 to explain the faded appearance of their new textiles. He worked for them for twenty-eight years.

Through his research, Chevreul articulated the "law of complementary contrast." This states that colors are affected by those that lie next to them. This effect had been observed since the Renaissance; Leonardo da Vinci was well aware of its impact in the fifteenth century, noting, "Each color is more distinctly seen, when opposed to its contrary, than to any other similar to it," but Chevreul took this premise further, developing the modern science of color theory. In the case of textiles, he was able to prove how colored yarns affect one another. A black line might appear green when surrounded by red—an instance of simultaneous contrast—or our brain might create the illusion of a line between different intensities of the same color.

Here, I've used the complementary pairs blue/orange and yellow/purple, which sets up a complementary contrast. These hues are helped along by contrast in lightness/darkness and temperature, so they engage us beyond passively looking: we see.

# Seeing Color

*Nature is a good colourist.*

—WILLIAM ROBINSON

## WHAT IS COLOR?

In 1666 Sir Isaac Newton had some mystical ideas about the number seven and so split the range of colors he saw in refracted sunlight into red, orange, yellow, green, blue, indigo, and violet. He published his findings under the title *Opticks* in 1704 and included a sketch of a color wheel meant to illustrate the range of colors he saw in white light.

But floral design, like painting, is about using color as expressed by (not through) a material thing—the flower itself, real and solid, clutched in your fingers. Take a red rose. The rose absorbs some colors from light and reflects red. As Kassia St. Clair explains in *The Secret Lives of Color*, "The color we perceive an object to be is precisely the color it *isn't*: that is, the segment of the spectrum that is being reflected away."

Chances are you already knew this, but it's important to remember that we don't always see light passing through a flower (though it is heavenly when we do). Thus, the materiality of our work means our struggles with color are painterly ones. Fine art, indeed!

Jessica Stewart explains on the website My Modern Met:

> First, we must understand that when our eyes look at something, light levels vary and they must take in a lot of information. This includes reflectance (how much light bounces off a surface), lightness (how our eyes perceive the reflectance), brightness (the perceived intensity of the light), and luminance (how intense the light is based on the sensitivity of our visual system).

Painters consider the various characteristics of color, so let's start by defining them:

**Value:** The quantity of light reflecting off a surface or the degree of lightness or darkness of a color relative to white or black.

**Hue:** What most of us mean when we refer to the name of a color, e.g., *orange*. Generally hue refers to a region of color on the color wheel.

**Temperature:** Colors can be classified as "warm" or "cool." Warm colors appear to come toward the viewer and even have been called "aggressive colors," while cool colors recede. For this reason, a red dahlia will appear larger than a purple one. It's useful to remember that temperature (like value) is relative and subjective, meaning that a flower may appear cooler or warmer (and recede or advance) depending on what sits next to it.

**Intensity/Chroma:** A measurable characteristic of color, intensity refers to the relative brilliance or dullness of a hue. Chroma refers to a color's purity or saturation. The two are related, but to avoid splitting hairs, I might use the terms interchangeably.

So what is color? Color is an experience. It is physically and psychologically experienced by the body and mind.

No wonder this is the longest section in the book.

UNDERSTANDING VALUE

Simply put, *value* is the term painters use to describe how much light something gives off. Differentiating between light and dark is fundamental to our survival—we wince and squint in bright light or open our eyes wider in the dark to take in necessary light and information. Our eyes can see about two hundred variations of value. Of course, every hue has a value, too, but let's start with the idea of contrast as it relates to value.

If you were to draw a picture of a ball on a table with a pencil, you'd probably sketch a circle on a line or square. To add dimensionality, you'd

FIGURE 1. Color wheel

FIGURE 2. Color temperature

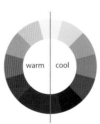

add shading–gradations of gray–to build up areas of dark and create contrast. That shading would create the illusion of a three-dimensional form, a ball as opposed to a circle. The gradations would create volume, and if you were really talented, we'd think we could pluck that ball right out of your picture. Why are we so easily deceived? As the eye moves from light to shadow, it interprets the lighter areas as closer and the darker ones as farther away. Thus, our brains make shape.

During the Baroque period, artists like Michelangelo Merisi da Caravaggio and Rembrandt van Rijn took advantage of the contrast of light and dark. The technique is called "chiaroscuro," pronounced *key-are-or-skewer-o,* and comes from the Italian words *chiaro* (light) and *scuro* (dark). Through the contrast of light and dark, these painters created drama. In Baroque painting, intricate detail, rich color, and heightened gesture all worked together to evoke emotion, but it was the use of light that defined the age.

So how can we apply these lessons to floral design? Of course, it's not as simple as black and white. We have to consider that every hue has a value, too.

Think of a simple red zinnia–a saturated variety like you'd find in a 'State Fair' mix. A real signal red. Such a hue would be of medium value. How so? Because neither white nor black have been added to that color.

Now think about the popular zinnia 'Queen Red Lime'. She leans burgundy and thus has a lower value than our purely red zinnia. By contrast, the petals of the new 'Queen Orange Lime' zinnia are lighter in temperature. Hence, we could say it has a higher value.

What might happen to these Queens in an arrangement? The Queen Red could disappear into shadows (or conveniently create them), and the Queen Orange the opposite–it would better stand out.

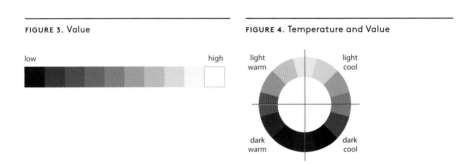

FIGURE 3. Value

low        high

FIGURE 4. Temperature and Value

light warm     light cool

dark warm     dark cool

High chroma *Rudbeckia hirta* with *Coreopsis* 'Incredible' Tall Mix, dahlias, zinnias, *Cosmos* 'Rubenza', and *Gladiolus* 'Bimbo'.

Now before this all seems too easy or intuitive, consider that the value of an object shifts relative to what lies next to it. You can make a flower appear lighter by having darker blooms around it and vice versa: surround a dark flower with paler ones, and it will be perceived as darker. This too often happens (to ill effect) in bridal work with rich, velvety blooms like chocolate cosmos, *Cosmos atrosanguineus*, and *Scabiosa atropurpurea* 'Black Knight'. They become black holes between paler flowers; unless surrounded with other low-value flowers, they disappear.

There's no question that some designers favor low-contrast work, while others opt for highly contrasted values. Take a look at the curated Instagram feed of any wedding photographer and you'll likely see a series of soft, pinky images with washed-out light and low-contrast flowers. Search foodie and floral hashtags like #darktable or #stilllifegallery to see how others create eloquence from the play of light and dark on a simple bowl of fruit.

If you're struggling with light and shadow in your work or want to know which details or colors might disappear, try taking a picture with your phone and converting it to black and white. This will allow you to see what's gained or lost.

In converting this picture to black and white, it's possible to see how similar the flowers are in terms of value and how our eyes are drawn to the areas of greatest contrast. Also note how the interplay of light and dark creates depth and volume, allowing us to see the work as layered, hummocky, complex.

# Monochromatic and Analogous Schemes

*It seems to me that color ought to be...embroidered on the canvas, that is to say, the same color ought to appear in the picture continually here and there, in the same way that a thread appears in an embroidery.*

—JAMES MCNEILL WHISTLER TO HENRI FANTIN-LATOUR, SEPTEMBER 30, 1868

### CONSTRAINING COLOR: MONOCHROMATIC SCHEMES

While monochromatic schemes may initially sound limiting, they offer tremendous opportunity for innovation and in my opinion are a fabulous training tool for beginners working with color. Rather than attempting daring combinations, choosing one hue forces us to really see the variations nature provides.

For example, say you'd like to work with yellow ochre because you have a fine chrysanthemum in that hue. Look closely at the flower. Does every petal display that color entirely? Chances are, no—the petals' backsides might curl toward buff or deepen to rust. It's this variation within the flower that can provide a cue to your composition.

In design terms, *monochromatic* refers to more than the use of a single color—it embraces tints, tones, and shades of a hue as well as temperature variations. In painting, a tint is a hue to which white has been added; a tone is one to which gray has been added; and a shade is the hue plus black.

How much white, gray, or black are added to a hue creates endless variations, but to simplify, using our ochre/chrysanthemum example, the tinted hue moves toward camel—or, in flower terms, the color of old dried hops. Yellow ochre with the addition of gray lands somewhere near light clay, the color of dried *Cecropia* leaves or the clean twig color of ilex

FIGURE 5. Tint, tone, and shade

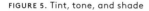
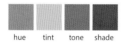

hue    tint    tone    shade

Narrowing your color choices offers an opportunity to play with tints, tones, and shades. Here, deep red plums with burgundy foliage provide a base from which hot pink, softer reds, and pinks emerge.

(winterberry). As a shade, the same ochre shifts greener toward olive, found in a wide range of foliage options like nandinas. There are countless botanical options, of course, but I hope these examples illustrate how a monochromatic design does not have to display the same precise color repeated by distinctively different plants.

Choosing to be purely monochromatic—using a single hue of red, say, such as red tulips with red amaryllises and roses—could be just the thing for a flamboyant floral frisson, but you can push other boundaries of style using color theory as a guide.


## ANALOGOUS COLORS

There's some confusion around monochromatic schemes, since many that are defined as such are, in fact, analogous. The word *analogous* comes from the ancient Greek *analogon* (proportionate). Before the digital world, before CDs vs. vinyl, *analogue* referred to something that was comparable to another.

An analogous scheme uses only one hue and its adjacent colors on the wheel—a single slice of the color pie. I often proceed in this manner, particularly if I have one great flower in bloom, such as a fresh ranunculus in a perfect plummy burgundy. Where to go with it? The answer is often right alongside that plum on the color wheel—from red-violet to purple to red.

Just as in a fine conversation, such segues serve to bridge ideas. We hold a flower in our hand, feel compelled by it, and look for similarities, relationships, echoes. Rather than leaping from hue to hue, analogous schemes conjure unity and harmony by making connections between colors.

FIGURE 6. Analogous colors

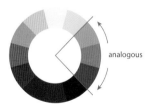

analogous

An analogous color scheme uses any shades, tints, or tones of colors that are within a 90-degree angle on the color wheel. The analogous colors apricot, saffron, buff, and salmon create a sense of unity in this arrangement of late-season hornbeam leaves and chrysanthemums.

A contemporary take on an analogous arrangement, this display of maple leaves, *Euonymus* 'Red Cascade', *Persicaria orientalis* (aka kiss-me-over-the-garden-gate), *Macleaya*, dahlias, and crab apples—all from the garden of Claus Dalby in Denmark—shows how starting with one signature plant (the maple in autumnal glory) can lead to a creative palette.

# Opacity and Luminosity

I love orange. I love the singe of it, its happy warmth, the way it brightens toward yellow and ages out to rust. You can get close to orange and touch it the way you can move your finger through a candle's flame and not get burned.

In this arrangement, there's not much true orange—peach and russet, with touches of pink, brown, yellow, white, and green. The orangest poppy here is *Papaver rupifragum* var. *atlanticum*, which sends up tall, wiry stems. The paler-peach poppy is an Icelandic, in this case 'Wind Song'. Ranunculus and stock fill in the spaces with pastels. A couple of tulips and white anemones tell me this is from May—a piece born of the lengthening days between spring and summer. I like that the arrangement stretches itself like late-spring light.

Given all the various oranges here, it's tricky to say why they work together so well. Yes, they are similar hues, which is always safe, but it's as if I'd taken an orange sorbet (or nasty 1970s sherbet) and added cream to create something softer on the senses. Adding white to a hue is called "tinting"; it lightens the color, but white can also add opacity.

Look closely at the Icelandic poppies: they look whitish with a yellow center. Their petals are actually white on the inside and orange on the back. That white flattens the light. The effect is a dulled orange, moving toward what we call "peach" (albeit an underripe one).

This opacity is mimicked in the ranunculus and dried bracken—crisp and dense, little light would pass through its leaves. In contrast, the clear petals of *Papaver atlanticum* glow like lollipops or gems in the light.

The term for this phenomenon is *luminosity*, which refers to brightness and radiance. As the English florist Janet Smith writes in the National Association of Flower Arrangement Societies handbook *Fundamentals of Colour*: "Luminosity is that attribute which denotes whether a color appears to emit or reflect more or less light and is determined, not by its hue or chroma, but by the quantity of reflected or emitted light."

We think of old oil paintings as being luminous—imagine an oyster or water droplet painted by a Dutch Master. The word dates from that period, traveling to French from the Old Latin *luminositas* (splendor). It later came to mean the intensity of light in a color, and I tend to think of the word in that way, muddling in the meaning from astrophysics, which uses luminosity to speak of the radiance of stars.

This arrangement uses primary colors to highlight the dynamism of a contrast of hue. Pictured: *Echinops*, sweet peas, poppies, coreopsis, *Cynoglossum*, *Helenium*, and 'Bishop's Children' and 'Waltzing Matilda' dahlias.

# Contrast

*Yellow with magenta is a clap of cymbals: once is exciting, twice is tolerable, but by the third you wish it would just stop.*
—NORI POPE

## WORKING WITH CONTRAST

*There's the rub.* How often do we use this expression to imply tension? We apply it to a situation that's a little tricky: a conflicting trade-off or a bit of unease we feel about an outcome of events. Color contrast is a rub—a complex one. A matter of science and perception, it has been used for centuries to manifest emotion.

Why does contrast matter so much to us as designers, painters, advertisers, and gardeners? Quite simply, the more something contrasts with its surroundings, the more visible it becomes.

Here are the seven forms of contrast, as developed by the Swiss artist Johannes Itten in his seminal 1961 book, *The Art of Color*:

**Contrast of Hue:** The three primaries—red, yellow, and blue—create visual interest through contrast when used together. The secondary colors—orange, green, and purple—create less, but the principle still applies.

**Contrast of Light and Dark:** A panda anemone—need I say more? I should, because that is a high-contrast flower and, as such, rare. As I mentioned in the section on value, you can use light and dark to create dimensionality. Remember—temperature influences value, too, and how we see light and dark can be influenced by context.

**Contrast of Temperature:** Warm and cool. Easy enough, but think about how a color might appear next to another; for example, a plummy

FIGURE 7. Contrast of temperature

warm on cool        warm on warm

hellebore like 'Anna's Red' will appear cooler next to orange than it would blue.

**Complementary Contrast:** In the nineteenth century, the French chemist Michel Eugène Chevreul (1786–1889) described how a color might appear depending on what colors lie next to it. In his book on color theory, *The Principles of Harmony and Contrast of Colors*, he wrote: "In the case where the eye sees at the same time two contiguous colors, they will appear as dissimilar as possible, both in their optical composition [hue] and in the height of their tone [mixture with white or black]."

This contrast is further pronounced when the colors are complementary. Colors that are perceptual opposites (yellow/violet, red/green, and blue/orange) create this contrast when juxtaposed. Claude Monet's *Chrysanthèmes rouges* uses saturated reds and greens in this way, and his purple agapanthus paintings accented with yellow show his understanding of the technique.

Van Gogh used complementary contrast to accentuate colors and convey intensity of emotion. Picture his brilliant cafe scenes or the colors in *Le semeur au soleil couchant* from 1888, where oranges, yellows, violets, and blues—to borrow from Itten—"incite each other to maximum vividness."

**Simultaneous Contrast:** In Itten's words: "Simultaneous contrast results from the fact that for any given color the eye simultaneously requires the complementary color, and generates it spontaneously if it is not already present." Stare long enough at a yellow box with a gray center (see figure 9), and eventually you will see a shimmer of purple where the gray once appeared.

While Chevreul's ideas and the Impressionists' use of complementary colors led to new ways of seeing (and painting) light, Neo-Impressionist painters used simultaneous contrast in exciting ways. Juxtaposing dots of color on the canvas, as opposed to blending color on a palette, meant

FIGURE 8. Complementary colors

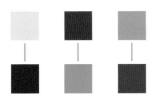

the viewer's perception composed the work. For example, in the work of Georges Seurat (1859–1891) and Paul Signac (1863–1935), whites are often created in our mind through the use of pure color. How? When complementary hues are optically mixed together, they form white. It is remarkable that colors so opposed can ultimately be subsumed in such a way, which is precisely what our brains do when we look at these paintings.

**Contrast of Saturation:** Imagine a display of spring tulips running from the pale peach 'Apricot Beauty' to the apricot 'Apricot Foxx' to a classic orange like 'Dutch Dancer' and finally to the brassy 'Brownie'. All contain orange but at different levels of saturation. Granted these botanical examples represent a contrast of value as well, but contrast of saturation plays with this scale.

**Contrast of Extension:** Think of this as the contrast between much and little (like proportion). The visual weight of a color matters to the idea of extension insofar as darker colors appear heavier and high intensity/chroma colors appear brighter. So how do we balance these: light/bright and dark/dull? In floristry we often assign proportions while in the midst of determining how a piece looks, but we can also plan ahead, knowing what we do about color value and chroma.

For example, say you'd like to work with a bunch of yellow tulips. These are light (value) and bright (chroma) flowers. Using the contrast of extension, you'd try to find that flower's opposite–something dark (value) and dull (chroma). Twigs fit that bill. But how many twigs would make the piece feel balanced? A surprising lot. Why? The light and bright flowers would need weighting down for the work to feel balanced, and so the proportion of twigs would increase.

Contrast of extension is highly subjective: just keep in mind that you have to balance colors proportionally to form a pleasing contrast.

FIGURE 9. Simultaneous contrast

FIGURE 10. Contrast of saturation

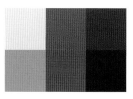

# A Study in Contrast

How do we so often forget what we know?

After indulging in a sugar-fueled fantasy of bulb ordering, one spring I found myself swimming in syrup—'Brown Sugar' and 'Brownie' tulips, to be precise. Brown tulips had been trendy the year before, and I loved their sweetness—that idea of autumn in spring displays.

I made this arrangement with a student named Tatiana Penner working alongside me. I had flown through my demonstration, using the sugary tulips low in the piece to ground the arrangement, some elegant *Amelanchier*, and the almost artichoke-like tulip 'Boa Vista' at the bottom left. After fifteen minutes, I was feeling rather smug…done!

But not. At. All.

A very sticky toffee pudding it was…

Meanwhile, Tatiana had quietly sunk into spring whites, snipping this and that from the garden, coolly carrying on, with me flitting in and out of her work. She was happy just to be playing with fresh cuts, having just emerged from a landscape of snow. I muddled along with my browns. A touch of peach, some white fritillaria, but barely pivoting on palette, nevertheless.

Eventually, we had two pieces to photograph, and one of them was clearly not working—my own.

I bustled between camera and vase, chatting and tweaking, and eventually Tatiana went outside. I squinted through the lens and finally remembered what it was that I knew: contrast can change everything. If I was facing the equivalent of a caramel-crusted custard, what might give such cloying sweetness levity? Blue sits across the color wheel from orange, making the two complementary. My confection needed frisson, tension. So in flew the butterflies (one of which had my answer right there on its wings), some Spanish bluebells and…whew.

TEN THINGS TO LEARN FROM IMPRESSIONIST
AND NEO-IMPRESSIONIST PAINTING

Art and art history have informed my work as a designer. Color, light, and movement are painterly concerns, and so studying paintings has helped me to see flowers in new ways. Here are some ideas gleaned from the work of the Impressionists and Neo-Impressionists that might inspire your work with flowers.

1. Your table is not just a surface but a plane. Make it work to draw your eye toward the vessel.
2. Shadow contains color.
3. Get outside. Make art from the art of nature.
4. Vessels designed for other purposes, such as jugs, crocks, and kitchen pottery, convey both warmth and craft.
5. Dots of color disappear at a distance, but when massed, the brain will create form.
6. Roadside flowers, "weeds," annual grasses, and wildflowers can be as beautiful as roses.
7. Choose flowers that possess gestural petals or sepals (like van Gogh's sunflowers or irises), curvy stems, or painterly qualities such as shaded coloration.
8. Work intuitively, not intellectually. Make it your job to convey the poetic qualities of light and color.
9. Backdrops and backgrounds matter. Choose textured or hand-painted materials.
10. Don't be afraid of color. The Impressionists favored yellow, orange, vermilion, crimson, blue, violet, and green.

# Seeing Red

*All my life I have found red a difficult colour.*
—CONSTANCE SPRY

Feeling a little hot under the collar? Rather be dead than red?

Clichés aside, in the warm months of summer, colors heat up. The harvest is nearing, colors deepening, berries ripening, and oranges, rubies, reds, and crimsons become the stars of the border and vase.

Red is a tricky color for some designers—garish? gaudy?—so for years many reserved it for the "hot border"—a sideshow to the main event of more conservative cool tones. In floristry, the color is all but forgotten after our literal saturation over Valentine's Day. But red is considered good luck in Chinese culture, and in Western culture it's historically the color of royalty, opulence, and majesty.

What flower really is red? I grow one truly red flower in the garden: an heirloom 'Red Spider' zinnia that leans neither orange nor purple. Almost all my other reds demand specificity: carmine, firecracker, vermilion, cerise...

Why is red so complicated? First of all, we can't easily see it. No, I don't mean the color blind (who are predominantly male)—I mean all of us. From a distance, red disappears. As Nori and Sandra Pope write in *Color by Design*, "At one yard red sings; at three yards, it is still pretty sonorous; at fifty, it is hard to differentiate from dark green shadows." Red absorbs most light. And for men (who, interestingly, have more rods in their eyes than women and thus cannot see subtleties of color as well as women but have better vision in low light and better depth perception), the qualities of red can be very hard to discern at a distance.

So, rule one: keep red close. Think of it this way—we all want to be warmed by a fire.

Rule two: it's more interesting to play across a color range than it is to juxtapose red with other colors. Picture this: blue ageratum, red zinnias, yellow cannas. All primaries, so a punchy combo for sure, but it sounds like a traffic-island planting, right?

Playing across a color range is more evocative. You might work oranges into scarlet, scarlet into crimsons, and crimsons into plums, exploring different tones and shades. I make a lot of bouquets and find the same strategies apply: harmonious, analogous groupings sell best. This doesn't mean they're simplistic—far from it. Rather, a range is expressed, so your eye doesn't jump from color to color and instead absorbs color, shape, and texture together—the subtleties of design.

Try incorporating burgundy and coppery foliage to create harmony when using red. For example, the popular dahlia 'Bishop of Llandaff' has dusky leaves and scarlet blooms, and the *Dianthus barbatus* 'Nigricans' group combines rich red blooms with dark foliage. I use the scented geranium *Pelargonium quercifolium* 'Chocolate Mint' in bold floral designs, given that it has velvety leaves with a nice "bruising" of purplish brown in the center of the leaves.

Green is directly across the color wheel from red, which means the two are technically complementary colors and thus create energy when used together. But contain that energy wisely: seek resonance of foliage and flower by leaning into deeper tones or muted surfaces. 'Blumex' and 'Rococo' parrot tulips exemplify this idea perfectly: matte sage-green leaves, saturated reds, and touches of burgundy and orange, all bundled into one wonderful plant.

# Using Green

*The objects in front of you are flowers, but the subject is color.*
—MICHELE COOPER

## ON GREENS

Greens and foliage are considered a category unto themselves in floral design. Used in most commercial designs (foliage is generally cheaper than flowers), the lack of diversity of plant material used might be explained by the longevity people have come to expect from standard bouquets.

Generally speaking, the leaves of commercial greens have a waxy cuticle that reduces transpiration, as is the case with myrtle, salal (*Gaultheria shallon*), eucalyptus, *Agonis*, *Grevillea*, and that staple of deli bouquets, leatherleaf (*Chamaedaphne calyculata*).

Looking back to earlier periods in the history of floral design has helped me to expand my range of foliage plants. With trial and error, almost anything goes for a short-lived display, but it's best to do some research about conditioning when experimenting with new plants.

Here's a short list of plants with beautiful foliage or forms, borrowed partly from William Robinson's 1883 book *The Wild Garden* and Gertrude Jekyll's 1907 book *Flower Decoration in the House*:

| | |
|---|---|
| acanthus (bear's breeches) | ilex (evergreen oak) |
| caladium | *Macleaya* (plume poppy) |
| *Corylus* (corkscrew hazel) | *Musa* (banana) |
| *Cotinus* (smoke bush) | *Onopordum* (cotton thistle) |
| *Crambe* (sea kale) | *Phytolacca* (pokeroot) |
| *Dipsacus* (teasel) | *Polygonatum* (Solomon's seal) |
| *Dryopteris* (male fern) | *Rheum* (rhubarb) |
| *Epimedium* (barrenwort) | *Ricinus* |
| *Ferula* (giant fennel) | *Verbascum* Mullein |

→ A late-summer collection of green squash and flowers, including *Nicotiana alata* 'Lime Green', *Amaranthus caudatus* 'Viridis', *Orlaya*, scabiosas, cosmos, dahlias, sweet peas, and 'Lacinato' kale

## GREEN FLOWERS

What is a sympathetic color?

A sympathetic person is one who listens before responding—a kind person, someone who will support us as we struggle to grow into ourselves. The same can be said of a green in a garden or floral arrangement. It acts as the supporter, the backdrop, and often as a tonic, too—green is the color of life-giving chlorophyll, fresh shoots, and growth. To borrow from *The Secret Lives of Color* by Kassia St. Clair, "In Latin the word for green is *viridis*, which is related to a large group of words that suggest growth and even life itself: *virere*, to be green or vigorous; *vis*, strength."

Green supports other colors, but it's also beautiful in its own right. As a secondary color, it includes a tremendous range of hues between the two primaries of yellow and blue. Consider these variations: chartreuse, pea, verdigris, emerald, avocado, olive, celadon, apple, absinthe, forest, mint, jade, kelly, sage...

Green flowers add life to arrangements. Here are some favorites:

1. Hellebores, including the *foetidus* and *viridis* groups.
2. Viridiflora tulips, which have green streaks on their petals, including the varieties 'Spring Green' and 'Green Spirit', both displaying a lovely combination of white/cream with green shading. (Speaking of green tulips, I adore the towering and long-lived 'Evergreen' and 'Boa Vista', a shiny artichoke of a flower with burgundy highlights.)
3. Spurges, including *Euphorbia polychroma* and *E. characias*. While the latter is almost a weed in my garden, I bow down before its chartreuse blooms in spring. Acidic and electric, this color will jump-start a palette.
4. In the same fresh color range as the *Euphorbia,* the summer annual cut flower *Zinnia* 'Envy'.
5. Other annuals, including the green nicotianas (*N. alata* group and *N. langsdorfii*). Both have spires of green, trumpet-shaped flowers that perk up dark palettes.

6.  Demure and enchanting, the perennial fringe cup *Tellima grandi-flora*, which works well in shade gardens, as does *Alchemilla mollis* (lady's mantle), a perennial with glaucous, felted leaves and singing yellow-green blooms. Alchemilla is a filler flower of the first degree and tough as can be. Like euphorbia and nicotiana, lady's mantle is tremendously useful for standing up to jewel tones and bright pinks. Dry it to tone down its brilliance; the color dulls to a mustardy gold.

7.  The cream-and-green *Gladiolus tristis*, a beautiful species recommended by Constance Spry.

8.  From the onion family, twisting garlic scapes and a range of sculptural flower buds. The wildest I've grown in this family is *Allium* 'Hair'.

9.  An offering from the carrot family, Queen Anne's lace cousin *Ammi visnaga* 'Green Mist', which is a soft Irish (aka kelly) green. Speaking of Ireland, another green summer wonder is the annual flower *Moluccella* 'Bells of Ireland', which is easily grown from seed and bends and swerves to a height of almost four feet in a season.

10. Amaranth, which is cultivated as a food crop and has long, draping flowers of pale green. Amaranth grows like a weed in warm weather and is spectacular spilling out of a vase.

11. *Viburnum opulus* (guelder rose). Its pale green, lace cap–like flowers work well with spring colors. Another green-flowering shrub is the uncommon *Itea ilicifolia,* which has elegant, pendulous inflorescences in early spring.

12. Trees offer gorgeous green flowers in spring. My favorite is the maple *Acer macrophyllum*, given its pure aplomb, but oaks, elms, avocados, and ash trees all offer quirky green-flowering stems.

# Stop and Go: Working with Red and Green

Oriental poppies have a sumptuousness that few flowers can match. At over five inches wide, with deep black stamens and a positively sexy stigma, they scream opulence. I began this arrangement with the single bloom of *Papaver orientale* 'Patty's Plum'. It's not truly a flower for cutting, but I wanted to capture its glory and bustled around the garden picking plants that mirrored it with either sheer sex appeal or color. Luckily, I had a rare ranunculus from the 'Super Green Porcelain' series, which is not porcelain-colored at all but loaded with shaggy swagger—the epitome of louche and an obvious mate for the wanton poppy.

The purple/burgundy foliage here—*Physocarpus* and elder—has enough depth to hold up to the poppy. That both shrubs were just beginning to bloom pink added some levity to the affair. There's more pink in here than you'd at first notice: the beautiful peony 'Coral Charm' at far right and a collection of ranunculus that shift from light pink to vermilion to plum.

But what really makes this piece work isn't solely the flowers. It's the vines—two types of clematises (the dark *C. montana* and the green, invasive traveler's joy, or *C. vitalba*). The green and red are in contrast to one another, so there's vibration, movement. The symbology here is worth thinking about: a red light says stop but a green says go.

Against a black backdrop, the darker plum flowers recede. I suppose this made me intuitively work harder to keep the green in the light. As for Patty the poppy, I believe those who cultivate mystery in order to ensnare others are best left to their silence.

# Color in the Age of Nuance

*The flower is charming by nature but* chic *only by fashion.*
—GEORGES MONTORGUEIL

If pastels were popular in the Rococo period—light lemon chiffons, shell pinks, and wide sky blues that matched the frivolity of the age—what does the love of muddied colors say of our time?

'Crème Brûlée' and 'Cherry Caramel' phlox, both deliciously muted, are now on trend. 'Cafe au Lait', a creamy beige dinner-plate dahlia, has been a top wedding flower for a few years. 'Antike' carnations and 'La Belle Époque' tulips are also the rage, the latter combining gold and pink into a smoldering buff. The hip 'Koko Loko' rose similarly demands painterly adjectives because it isn't truly any one color: it's lavender, pinkish, and butterscotch-ish. Popular dyed flowers—roses, sweet peas, tulips, and peonies—look as if tea-stained with brown.

What happened to pure color? Have we all been shaded, tinted, and toned?

My cutting garden feels like a horticultural ice cream parlor some days. I'm growing 'Hot Chocolate' nicotianas, 'Chocolate' cosmos (*C. atrosanguineus*), 'Seaton's Toffee' chrysanthemums, and 'Brownie' and 'Brown Sugar' tulips, and I'm on the hunt for *Heuchera* 'Caramel' and 'Tiramisu', despite already owning 'Ginger Ale', 'Mai Tai', and 'Marmalade'. If I were better organized, I'd be looking forward to rich, brown bearded irises burnished with apricot, which are having a renaissance, given their somber hues.

In this age of health-conscious abstention, do we now drink our greens and indulge in visual desserts?

A couple of years ago I visited Sarah Raven's garden at Perch Hill in England. She's known for her 1996 book *The Cutting Garden*, as resplendent and colorful as they come ("Venetian" is how she describes her past palette of choice). *The Cutting Garden*'s style brings to mind the other gardening books of that age: *The Jewel Garden: A Story of Despair and Redemption* by Monty and Sarah Don and Thomas Hobbes's *The Jewel Box Garden*. Euphorbias glowed in these books, and garden rooms glittered

with rich maroons, poignant purples, striking raspberries, and brilliant oranges. Raven even had periwinkle-blue posts erected in her garden for one more hit of color. The gardeners of this generation, only a few years prior to my own, I admit, colored their way onto a bright floral stage.

And now? In more ways than one, we've entered the age of nuance.

Look at a wedding today: where bold masses of color once stood, gradations now flow. Ombré is in.

Movement and texture seem to matter more than color. I once heard the lovely, trendsetting Anna Potter of the British flower shop Swallows & Damsons say (echoing John Ruskin), "Anything that isn't a color is my color."

Perhaps we can blame the new naturalism in garden design: those wafting waves of smoky seed heads and undulating, desiccated grasses. Or perhaps it was the advent of camera phones, which struggled with saturated colors. Or perhaps plant breeding offers up ever more variety to insatiable gardeners. As the British novelist Penelope Lively recently wrote, "Garden fashion depends upon what there is available to become fashionable." I only hope we can do more than just desserts.

# Tone on Tone

The phrase *tone on tone* is currently trending in fashion and interiors. The idea is to play with variations of one hue and its tints, shades, and tones. The trend includes using variations of one color for a complete outfit, room, or even house. One might play across a whole range of colors in a certain family. Mrs. Shell Pink and her coral daughter, peachy son, and rosy husband. You get the idea.

In gardening, we might call this a "color-themed" planting scheme, while knowing, as flower people do, that nature adores variation. For example, say you'd like to create a calming corner of cool-colored plants or an arrangement of the same. Your central hue would be blue, but you'd tone into pastels and shade toward indigo. What might such a scheme look like in terms of flower selection?

In spring: *Muscari*, *Scilla*, 'Blue Diamond' tulips, anemones, *Brunnera* (forget-me-nots), and early irises. In summer: the wonderful bee plant *Phacelia*, hardy geraniums, baptisias, lupines, polemoniums, nepetas (catmint), *Cerinthe*, borages, delphiniums, sweet peas, nigellas (love-in-a-mists), and clematises. In late summer, you could still keep cool by dipping into the pale blues and purples of *Echinops* (globe thistle), lavenders, or the silver blues of *Eryngium*. Annual linums (flax) are a fine, clear blue, while larkspurs are available in smoky blues and purples. Come August, verbenas, lisianthus, and heliotropes can take the heat. In autumn, *Salvia patens, pratensis,* and S. 'Phyllis' Fancy' and 'Black and Blue' would carry the theme into October, as would the towering deep blue aconite.

In this arrangement, made with my student Eunkyung Kil, raspberry pink forms the central hue, which deepens to burgundy in the ranunculus and hellebores. The gerbera daisies appear dulled or toned, as if gray had been added to raspberry, while the anemones and 'Ariadne' butterfly ranunculus show how tinting with white shifts the raspberry to a light pink. The veining of the sweet peas and the dyed 'Brownie' tulips offer variation on this theme.

# PART FOUR

# SHAPING
# YOUR WORK

# This Time with Feeling

*A regulating line is an assurance against capriciousness.... It confers on the work the quality of rhythm.*
—LE CORBUSIER

The early twentieth-century American painter Charles Hawthorne (1872–1930) once quipped, "Let color make form—do not make form and color it," which may be true enough for painting, but florals are three-dimensional works. We could say that, technically, they have both a shape (as in an outline) and a form, because an arrangement has height, width, and depth.

Line also plays a role in design: consider a flower aloft on a stem. How does the line of its stem initiate aesthetic response? How does its width, direction, and length alter perception and emotion? What's the effect of having a flower look straight at you versus demurely away? A gracefully drooping tulip, fully blown, says something altogether different than a perky poppy or hanging *Amaranthus*.

In this section, I will explore the dance of the flowers. I'll draw on the fine arts to consider motif, gesture, movement, mass, balance, and rhythm, dipping into a bit of stagecraft, dance, sculpture, music, and history along the way.

But first: flowers. Flowers themselves have mass, volume, line, and shape. They take up space and yet also visually create it. Tactile and textural, they are the raw materials we sculpt with. But flowers also come in myriad forms, sizes, styles, and colors, so let's start with the basics.

← Circles on circles. This spring arrangement of ranunculus, anemones, tulips, poppies, and *Choisya* is one of my favorites. Why does it work? The flowers are balanced in the vase, facing forward, but save for a few blooms, they aren't looking directly at the viewer. We aren't affronted by effusive optimism, despite the cheery tableau. We're greeted by only a few flowers looking our way and, as when walking into a well-hosted party, we feel welcome to get to know the others in our own time.

Gesture, line, mass. So many considerations influence design. This arrangement, made with Becky Feasby, uses *Agastache*, watermelon-red hollyhocks, 'Madame Butterfly Bronze' snapdragons, and the dahlias 'Islander' and 'Labyrinth' to create depth and weight. Hops and clematises do the gestural work, while the yellow *Rudbeckia* 'Herbstonne' offers piquancy.

# Considering Flowers

*Nature is perhaps the most complex word in the language.*
—RAYMOND WILLIAMS

## FLOWER PARTS

What is a flower? To an insect, food. To a plant, the future. To us, it depends on our purposes. We eat flowers, rely on them for seed, admire them, extract scents from them, heal with them, and convey messages of loss, love, and hope through them.

With flowers carrying so many cultural associations, it's no wonder humans have shaped them through breeding to deliver what we want, be it black tulips or stuffable squash blossoms. But a flower's qualities (shape, scent, and color) were originally formed by the sensory perceptions of the insects who pollinated them.

It's important to understand a flower's basic parts, so we'll dive into a little botany with the caveat that nature is more nuanced than what I'll have space to discuss. Let's examine the decorative structures of flowers:

**Petals:** Often the showiest parts of a flower, they assume many shapes, from fused, tubelike blooms (salvias) to elongated rays (daisies) to folded confections (sweet peas) to circular collections (hollyhocks and poppies).

**Calyces (sing. Calyx):** An often green, brown, or leaflike outer layer (think cardoons or artichokes), sometimes divided into sepals.

The calyx and petals of a flower usually form what is referred to as the corolla—the parts of the flower surrounding the reproductive organs.

**Sepals:** Leaflike elements that usually function to protect flowers, wrapping around them in bud and later supporting the petals. In plants such as narcissus, amaryllis, and some lilies, the distinction between sepals and petals isn't clear. In these cases, the petallike sepals are called tepals. In both anemones and clematises, sepals appear petallike.

**Bract:** A kind of modified leaf that may be decorative. This is the case in bougainvillea and poinsettia; the bracts are showier than the flowers but serve a similar goal—to attract pollinators. In arums the showy bract is called a spathe.

**Stamens:** The male organs of flowers, which are composed of filaments and anthers (the latter carry the pollen). On shrubs such as witch hazel and trees such as acacia and *Callistemon*, stamens are a decorative feature.

**Pistil:** The female reproductive portion of a flower, composed of an ovary, ovule, style, and stigma. When the stigma is fertilized, the ovary of a plant swells in the formation of seed. Rose hips and crab apples are examples of floral ovaries.

### FLOWER SHAPES

Why smile like a daisy when you can seduce like a svelte foxglove? From the flower's perspective, it depends on whom you're trying to attract, but from our perspective we might consider the mood of a piece when choosing flower shapes. Vertical spikes and spires create energy and uplift in a design, while circles are often cheery and bowl-shaped flowers like peonies and roses signal abundance and romance (to me).

Flower shapes vary dramatically by family, and botanists have specific terms to categorize them, but for our sake general terms will suffice. Here are some common shapes:

**Panicles or Clusters:** Often used as filler flowers; examples include hydrangeas and phlox.

**Balls/Globes:** *Craspedia*, *Echinops*, and some dahlias form spheres. The onion family also provides us with a range of balls and ovals.

**Umbels:** While yarrows, angelicas, and sedums supply flat blocks of color, other umbel-shaped flower clusters like those of dill, fennel, cow parsley, and *Bupleurum* are lacier.

**Plumes:** Astilbe and celosia are two common plumes used in floral design. Perennials such as filipendulas and grasses like pampas grass and *Pennisetum* are also plume shaped.

**Bell-Shaped:** Campanulas are also known as bellflowers, but a number of other flowers assume this shape, including *Cobaea*, fritillaria, and some varieties of clematis.

**Spikes:** These exclamation points of the flower world include *Liatris*, kniphofias, and delphiniums.

**Spires:** Digitalises, *Agastache*, salvias, and larkspurs all fall in this category.

**Circles:** Certain flowers appear as circles or dots, including poppies, anemones, scabiosas, and ranunculus.

**Daisy-Shaped:** This not-very-scientific-sounding term describes flowers with rays in the *Asteraceae* family, including sunflowers, rudbeckias, heleniums, and echinaceas.

**Trumpet-Shaped:** The amaryllis and lily are the most obvious, but on a smaller scale, petunia and salpiglossis also are examples of this group.

**Bowl or Cup-Shaped:** Ranunculus, roses, and peonies all exhibit this form.

# Texture

*Nothing sticks to a smooth surface. A certain roughness,*
*and ugliness even, is required in our creative lives.*
—ERIC WEINER

There comes a point in autumn when fruit eclipses root. When we stop watering and start ripening—the tomatoes we push, squashes we harden, and flowers we encourage to set seed.

The garden appears to lean into autumn's golden light, almost as if knowing how beautiful it will look: a swan song in soft sun, followed by a brilliant feint as the light strikes cobwebs and calyces. And suddenly, as if we hadn't been paying attention, we notice it all: the last shining blackberry, a backlit orange leaf, the powdery duff of a quince.

Texture means many things to an arrangement; relief, light, softness, and also the inverse: clarity. Silhouettes slip into focus in the fall, and there's a cinematic romance to the season, almost as if we see our world side lit—the sun's glow close enough to draw our attention to a subject and yet diffuse enough to blur a scene.

Can you tell I am smitten by the season? This feeling supports my autumnal gardening fatigue, of course. The garden and I are both healthily resigned in October. The plants have run their course, I've done my best, and all spring's hope is finally exhaled.

What we as gardeners have forgotten to do—cut back, pick, yank, weed—is there to see but no longer glaring. Fog ices our cake.

Every autumn, I return to teach at the Cambo Estate in Scotland, where low-angled light and mist are as much a part of the success of the garden as the plant choices, which play to the Scottish weather. Seed heads are left standing until February to catch the dew and frost. Grasses arch, softening vistas, creating mystery, veiling burgundies, purples, and yellows. Garish asters and scorching rudbeckias are set to simmer behind a haze of seeds.

Yes, I like to see plants age in place; I also know it's better for the health of gardens and the critters that feed and shelter in them if they do.

Texture—of leaf, flower, fruit, and seed head—is of primary concern in fall arrangements. Deep brown spires of perennials become sculptural, heavier, capable of balancing the saturated colors of foliage. We can use fruits, nuts, and vegetables in designs invoking the spirit of harvest time, again expanding the range of textures in our work.

## FLOWER QUALITIES

Plants adapt not only to insects through flower shape, scent, and style but also to environments. A delicate flower would not last long in a dripping rain forest nor emerging from snow. The tremendous diversity of flower qualities means we can find flowers and plants for every lighting situation and mood. As you skim this somewhat limited list, consider how the interplay of flower qualities might enliven your work.

**Shiny**
anthurium, butterfly ranunculus, holly, ivy, monstera leaves, philodendron, tomato

**Fleshy/Waxy**
amaryllis, calla, cup and saucer vine, heliconia, hyacinth, lily, magnolia, orchid, young tulips

**Diaphanous**
abutilon, feather-top grass, fiber optic grass, Icelandic and Shirley poppies, lunaria

**Matte**
anemone, carnation, dahlia, hellebore, Japanese anemone, lilac, marigold, nasturtium, nicotiana, palm, ranunculus, rose, zinnia

**Glaucous**
eucalyptus, figs, fritillaria, grapes, kale, opium poppy pods and foliage, peas, sempervivums, and many succulents

**Felted**
bunny tail grass, dusty miller, lamb's ears, pelargonium, *Plectranthus*, *Salvia argentea*

# Gesture

Excuse me? Waiter? Could you...please?

The crooked finger, the upheld arm, the eyebrows lifted...How do we invite someone in for a conversation? A word?

Through gesture.

*Gesture* is a term used throughout the arts—we refer to a painting as gestural when the brushstrokes appear vigorous, free, and expressive. In gesture drawing, an artist tries to capture movement or disposition. In music, gesture implies a kind of physical and aural coherence.

As the music critic Edward Rothstein writes, "Music played without gesture is like a person speaking with a rigidly held body; music played with artificial gestures is like a person gesticulating wildly while humming a lullaby."

In floral design, an artificial gesture might look like a single flower popping up from a mass—a periscope effectively submarining your design. A design lacking gesture might appear stiff and overly formal.

The American sculptor John Chamberlain once said, "It just can't be a blob sitting there. It should be doing something."

We animate floral designs through gesture. We might create motion through curving lines, a feeling of expansion through angles, or a sense of fluidity through close attention to the shape of our materials. Sculptural beginnings and endings can offer the viewer a type of narrative with an exciting entrance and satisfying denouement.

Because I don't do much large-scale installation work and I draw from my strengths as a gardener, I find it easiest to think in terms of gestural flowers and plants before I begin a design. These are often naturally wavy plants like foxgloves, Bells of Ireland, vines, or lighter blooms with thin stems. These dancers might invoke attention, stretching beyond the work to create negative space. They needn't necessarily be outliers, so long as they engage the eye: the more our eyes move around a piece to appreciate it, the more enthralled we become. (But a caveat: only to a point. A work that gesticulates wildly, that lacks coherence, turns most of us off.)

So how do we find that balance?

Think of gesture the way some dancers do: as movements that do not carry the weight of the whole body (or your whole arrangement, unless you have tremendous range for your commission and the vision to sustain a fully choreographed work, such as a burrow of branches or an aisle or arbor). Consider familiar human movements and their meanings: the difference between a hand proffered and a hand withheld or the implications of a wrist flexed and a head cocked. What do these gestures say? All of these movements suggest meaning and emotion, and though I can't quite go so far as to say a looping vine of bittersweet can be read the way the human body can, I often prefer an arrangement where the flowers appear to be in conversation with one another.

In the early days of Dutch still life painting, most flowers faced the viewer. Later, the paintings became more complex, with the backs of petals shown and flowers turned. Flowers gestured at one another and the viewer, inviting engagement.

These days we're all familiar with ejaculatory pampas grass, floral clouds, and the curved sleekness of a cycad leaf as used in modernist work. These may speak to some, but their success depends on the overall design. Thus, it's difficult to be prescriptive about gesture—your flowers and plants either have sway over the viewer or they don't.

But even if they don't literally sway, you can fake it. You might build a frame of chicken wire that embodies movement and lace straight-necked plants into it; you can twist a vine, curve a young sappy branch, or simply bend a straight tulip's stem between your fingers.

Floral design is a silent art, but, as in dance, gesture can function as a vocabulary. We speak through our designs.

← Some plants naturally create gestures; others you can manipulate to create swoops and bends. Tulips are phototropic, meaning that they bend toward light. They can also be warmed, stretched, and curved by gently stroking their stems and adding pressure in the direction of your choice. (Tulip petals, like rose petals, can also be flexed for effect). Other gestural plants include Icelandic poppies, foxgloves, *Moluccella* 'Bells of Ireland', fritillaria (*F. meleagris* pictured here), amaranth, grasses, and of course vines (to name only a few). With solid mechanics, it's easy to create drama and gesture with few flowers.

# Form

*When the whole and the parts are seen at once, as mutually producing and explaining each other, as unity in multeity, there results shapeliness*—forma formosa.

—SAMUEL TAYLOR COLERIDGE

## THE GOLDEN RATIO

Time to put your math hat on (if you have one—if you don't, we'll muddle forward together) to examine an ancient concept in mathematics and aesthetics: the Golden Ratio.

This term, developed in the 1800s, was essentially a renaming of Leonardo da Vinci's sixteenth-century ideas on divine proportion. You've seen the sketch, I'm sure: a man with arms upheld in a square surrounded by a circle. Da Vinci and other artists used the divine proportion in their pursuit of beauty and balance in sculpture and painting.

So what exactly is this divine proportion? And what does it mean for floral design?

Consider the questions we face: How many of one plant do we blend with another? How tall should an arrangement be?

To address the latter question, we'll begin with an easy proportion to visualize: vase to flowers. The old rule of thumb is to build an arrangement two-thirds higher than your vessel. To state it another way: look at your flowers and choose a vessel one-third their height. This loosely follows the golden geometry of proportion, which can be expressed mathematically as 1.618, or phi. Even our bodies are roughly sized to this proportion. I'm conventionally shaped, and the distance from the top of my head to the tips of my fingers is about two-thirds of my total height.

← The issue of numbers plays into the design principle of color blocking. In floristry, this refers to using one color en masse, as opposed to dotting it throughout the design. Blocks of color (sometimes represented by the same flowers) can be used together to make a work feel more cohesive and dynamic. Think of the difference between printed and solid-color clothing: patterning creates busyness and can diffuse color and reduce contrast, while blocks of color appear strong. Here, a holiday arrangement of *Magnolia grandiflora* leaves, cedar, spruce, nerine, anemone, statice, and winterberry uses mass and blocking for impact.

Now that we have height solved, what about volume? What's the Golden Ratio there? How much foliage should a bouquet have? How many flowers of a certain form can be used with another?

In order to answer this, I need to introduce another mathematician: Fibonacci, who in 1202 wrote the book *Liber Abaci*, outlining a mathematical progression that is now known as the Fibonacci sequence—a series of numbers that begins 0, 1, 1, 2, 3, 5, 8, 13, 21, 34....(He wasn't the first to articulate the magic of this math; it had already been recognized in ancient Hindu culture.) Each new number in the sequence is the sum of the two before it. So: 0+1=1, 1+1=2, 1+2=3, 2+3=5, 3+5=8, and so on. As those numbers increase, the ratio of each number to the one before it approaches...phi.

You can see why people have been obsessed with phi for centuries, imbuing it with almost metaphysical meaning. Nature is rife with the expression of Fibonacci numbers, as they are called: a sunflower's seeds present in a spiral of these numbers, as do echinaceas. Passionflowers follow Fibonacci sequencing...Just google "mathematical plant pattern sequencing," and you'll be seeing divine order in no time.

But let's come down to earth: you want to help a friend do her wedding flowers. You have to do some calculations. How many of this and how many of that? This is obviously a matter of personal taste—do you want something floriferous, or something more leafy?—so it's very difficult to generalize, and a flower recipe book may work best as a guide. But for the sake of trying, let's see if Fibonacci sequencing can help get proportions right.

Say you've got centerpieces to do. You will need focal flowers, gestural flowers, filler flowers, foliage, and, in my world, seedy bits or surprises. Try applying the sequence: five showy dahlias for focal flowers, eight stems of cosmos for gesture, thirteen bits of stock for filler, and twenty-one snippets of *Artemesia* for foliage. Not a bad start!

(A practical aside: When making table pieces, remember people need to talk over them, so lean your elbow on the table and make a fist beside your arrangement. The top of your hand is your maximum height.)

# Threes, Fives, and Sevens

A dictum of contemporary garden design and, to some extent, floral design is to work in odd numbers—threes, fives, sevens, and so on. Odd numbers suggest the spontaneity of nature, which rarely presents itself in matching sets. Place two poppies on either side of an arrangement, and it grows eyes because our brains are hardwired for facial recognition. Add a third or fifth poppy off-center, and you subvert the brain's need to form patterns.

If viewers can't easily find a pattern in your work—pairs of plants or flowers—their eyes move around a design and experience more of it.

Dynamism is preferred over static, regimented displays (depending on the setting, of course—not in a formal garden or period-style arrangement).

So, to count stems or not? I don't count flowers as I work because I don't have

to—often, I just pick what I need from the garden. But scarcity is real for me, too. I'll use two matching flowers if they'll do, four if I have them, and ten if they are called for. And yes, even one of a very special kind.

Flowers vary in size, quality, and shape, whether purchased or grown. You'll find a solid grounding in techniques and aesthetics offers the best foundation for artful design, and, like a well-trained chef cooking without a recipe, you'll be better prepared to improvise. Think about the numbers game like you might measure your weight or shape: there are no easy formulas for what makes someone or something beautiful.

That said, if you aren't sure why an arrangement isn't working, count your blooms. Ask yourself: Is the piece too balanced, too static? Then add or subtract.

→ A New York mash-up of lotus, *Asplenium*, banana flowers, kumquats, tulips, hellebores, ranunculus, and *Fritillaria imperialis*, made with Ursula Gunther.

## SYMMETRY AND ASYMMETRY

Most humans are bilaterally symmetrical, with pairs of eyes, ears, legs, et cetera, and most people respond positively to well-balanced faces. It follows that people tend to like a certain balance and equilibrium in art.

A traditional symmetrical arrangement achieves balance through the replication of a shape, almost as if a line were drawn down the middle of the composition and the same design elements applied to each side. Balance, in this example, is achieved through matching scale, proportion, and shape.

But symmetrical designs aren't always balanced. Recalling our discussion of color, we may have an arrangement that is bilaterally similar but visually unbalanced. If one side has a dark mass of purple and the other a more bright lavender, we might feel the balance to be off due to the heaviness or lightness of color.

Similarly, asymmetry doesn't preclude the idea of balance. We interpret an asymmetrical design or painting to be balanced when we feel each side has a similar visual weight. One example of this might be when small areas of vibrant color are balanced by larger areas of neutrals.

In terms of form, a strong line might also balance a mass. Picture a seesaw with the fulcrum way over to one side. How might it balance? With something small on the longer arm and a large mass on the short end, balancing the weight. This technique can be particularly helpful with top-heavy blooms on long stems, like French tulips. While they might reach out from a design, creating movement, they often need visual counterweight to balance the piece.

# Rhythm and Repetition

Floral design, at its most basic, is the pulling together of parts into a unified whole. Composers orchestrate a score and decide what and how many instruments are needed, while florists might budget a set amount of focal flowers, foliage, and trailing plants per vase.

But looking at a finished arrangement, what is it that creates rhythm? Most of us like the idea of harmony, though what really is it? It's simply sounding more than one note in a way considered pleasant. In floral design, it might be achieved through a repetition of texture, color, or shape. Not everyone wants harmony, of course, but it's wise to know how to create it.

I'm going to introduce a word that fascinated me the second I learned it because I'd had no way to describe why I loved a certain piece of music, and I couldn't rest until I figured out why. And the second I learned the term, I knew it applied to floristry.

The term is *ostinato*, which describes a continued musical motif, phrase, or rhythm. The word comes from the Italian word for "stubborn." (I like the term as applied to concert music best because I think the *ost* of *ostinato* is aptly guttural sounding, deep-throated, and earthy; in pop music you could use a repeating riff to function in a similar way.)

In Baroque music, when the bass keeps repeating the same line or chords, it is called *basso ostinato*, or ground bass, and no piece of music better exemplifies it than *Canon in D Major* by Johann Pachelbel. Listen to it, and immediately you'll hear the bass. Violins play over and around that line, but the bass ground remains. What effect this has on you might relate to how many times you've heard the piece of music; Pachelbel composed it in the late seventeenth or early eighteenth century, but after a popular recording was released in 1968, it became so ubiquitous during my youth that it lost its appeal. I now value it because it exemplifies how complexity can increase within a framework of repetition. The *basso ostinato* sustains us through thrilling variations.

Almost every star needs a supporting cast, every poignant lyric a refrain. So what do you need or want to be stubbornly present in your work?

129

For me, it's often what I have the most of because, honestly, abundance demands my attention. If you were a chef, you'd build a menu from all the peas ripening in your garden. You'd puree some, blanch some, build a dish with variations on that pea theme. Repetition of flavor, if not texture, might reign.

Try to create rhythm through the repetition of a key color, shape, or texture. And look to gardens, too, because mastering repetition is precisely what naturalistic plantings do.

The landscape designer Piet Oudolf's naturalistic perennial plantings helped form the basis of the Dutch Wave landscaping movement that came to prominence in the 1990s. He's the man behind the design of the High Line in New York, and his work can be viewed around the world. One of his signatures is the use of grasses to create veils/hazes through which light passes; seed heads and flowers can be seen through these screens or highlighted against them. He uses masses of perennials in drifts, but there's often tremendous variation in plant heights, colors, and shapes. He thinks in shape and silhouette. What makes the designs so effective is their rhythm, particularly in autumn. Built from repeating bass notes of gold, russet, and brown and repeating plant forms, they express just enough harmony to soothe and just enough variation to keep us interested.

Take a look as well at the large-scale modernist work of the New York floral designer Emily Thompson. Blooms appear within or emerge from woody structures that she weaves. Thompson's penchant for branchy browns has a similar effect to Oudolf's grasses—a marked repetition of color and texture from which surprises spring, much like Pachelbel's violins. Flowers dance around the weightiness of the work. What may look like a tangle of branches loosely assembled around flowers becomes art when the viewer brings perception and emotion into the mix. Instead of simply flowers and twigs, we might see a nest studded with multicolored eggs, a hedgerow bursting with wildflowers, or even a cloud filled miraculously with stars.

Rhythm is produced when you repeat certain patterns or create parallels. In speech, we might think of political rhetoric's power to evoke emotion through the repetition of words and phrases; in floral design, it's easy to create rhythm through repeating textures and colors. In this piece I created with Jing Harris, dried plants function as a ground, with dried hops woven throughout the bouquet. The ferns (*Sticherus*) are sadly bleached before being lightly plasticized, but here they help to lift the browns to cream. The two natural grasses, *Briza* and *Lagurus*, repeat the refrain.

# Exit Stage Left

The floral designer Max Gill studied theater before turning to flowers. He taught me a valuable lesson: in Western culture we read a work from left to right. Of course, I had known this intuitively, but I'd never thought of it in design terms and I'd certainly not thought of flower arrangements as being enacted as a play might be on a stage. But we do demand that flowers perform—on pedestals, mantels, and altars; we expect drama, so in many ways the same rules apply. Stagecraft often is what a florist does, whether at the level of a large installation or a simple centerpiece. We harness beauty and emotion and present it on a stage of space.

I loved Max's idea; the more I thought about it, the more I understood how hundreds, if not thousands, of years of history have changed how we see.

Take a look at the large orange-and-white 'A la Mode' dahlia at the lower right of this arrangement. What's it doing there? Anchoring a corner? Yes. Drawing our attention with its sheer size and smiling, blown face? Sure. Now imagine a spotlight shining down on its petals as if it were on a stage. What might it say? Would it tell you a tale about all the flowers behind it? Might it lean intimately into your space?

This dahlia is in the position an actor conventionally takes for a soliloquy. It cozies up to us, whispers a few secrets, and for a moment steals the show. So pay heed to that area. Save it for a star.

But how does such an actor fade out of our attention? Traditionally, he or she will "exit stage left." (It might take a moment to decode this familiar line because playwrights refer to the view we see in the audience in the reverse. "Stage left" is to an actor's left—and the viewer's right.)

Truthfully, I was a bit gobsmacked to see how many of my arrangements start with a bang on the left and fade out to the right. I just naturally trail off in that direction, trained by my culture to read left to right and signal the end of an act.

# PART FIVE

# LEARNING
# FROM
# THE PAST

# Baroque Style

*Any great work of art…revives and readapts time and space, and the measure of its success is the extent to which it makes you an inhabitant of that world—the extent to which it invites you in and lets you breathe its strange, special air.*
—LEONARD BERNSTEIN

When I first developed the outline for this book, I omitted the Baroque. Why would such a significant period in history—in art, music, architecture, and, yes, flowers—be overlooked? I was stunned once I noticed my omission, but I suspect it was like stepping out into the garden on a glorious spring day and forgetting to think about the sun.

The sun is a fitting image, not solely because of the Sun King, Louis the XIV, who reigned in the Baroque, but because so many of the ideas born in that age have affected how we now see, hear, and navigate the world.

The word *baroque* comes from the Portuguese word *barroco*, which refers to a pearl of irregular shape. Initially the term implied bad taste—something overdone or bizarre, overwrought. We no longer associate irregularity with designs of the period: luxury, opulence, detail—sure, but symmetry won over disorder, beauty and order over chaos.

Why? It's important to remember that the Baroque overlaps with the Enlightenment. For all the drama of the age, all the exuberance in art and music, the period between the early seventeenth and late eighteenth century was also an era of intense commercialism, increased secularization, and scientific inquiry.

René Descartes, David Hume, Sir Isaac Newton, and countless others wrote in the fields of natural philosophy and science. Johann Sebastian Bach composed works of profound emotional impact, expressing great complexity of rhythm, harmony, and structure. Carl Linnaeus developed scientific nomenclature late in the Baroque as plants flooded into Europe on ships, developing the genus/species binomials we now use every time we read a plant tag or order flowers. All shaped aesthetic understanding.

So picture yourself in peak Baroque architecture, in the famous hall of mirrors at Versailles. Decorative? Indeed. Those grand chandeliers, the scrolls of gilding, the light, reflection, and opulence. A touch extravagant? Yes. Dazzling? Wonderfully so.

My first visit to the hall was at ten o'clock on a hot summer's evening. I had expected to be overwhelmed by beauty, and I was (not least of all by the period music, as I was there for a private concert), but I also felt strengthened by the grandeur because there was a clear, logical flow to the room, with repetition and symmetry providing structure to its design (as well as to the music). Versailles shows us that harmony was just as important to the age as the grand embellishments we think of as Baroque.

So what does this mean for floral design? Abundance, certainly, but also control. As Margaret Fairbanks Marcus says in *Period Floral Arrangement*, "The mood of the baroque is dynamic and boldly confident.... The final effect should be neither rigid nor bunched, but voluptuous and graceful."

Colors popular in the period included rich reds, gold, blues, Chinese yellow, mint and emerald green, and strawberry pink.

Now, in terms of actual plants, consider what was happening in European exploration during the Baroque. Dutch ships continued to make Amsterdam a great power even after the tulipomania that gripped its economy in the early seventeenth century. Flowers such as sweet peas (originally from Sicily), nasturtiums (from Peru), amaranth (from the Americas), and Chinese asters (*Callistephus chinensis*) arrived in Europe in the early eighteenth century, along with Oriental poppies, agapanthus, kniphofias, *Verbena bonariensis*, and *Magnolia grandiflora*.

French, Dutch, Spanish, and English colonies continued to be established around the globe. Botanic gardens sprung up as plant collectors returned from China, Africa, North America, Indonesia, and the Caribbean with specimens. New species arrived daily. Painters and engravers documented the bounty, and their floral works loosened in style during the period.

And passion—for art, for nature—grew more individualized. As knowledge of the natural world flooded onto the continent and humanism arose from the thinkers on European soil, people were allowed to love a single flower as a manifestation of God's magnificence. Radical, at the time. The investigations of petal and sepal, the counting of stamens and anthers, the exacting empiricism, even the delicacy of a painted broken tulip, were means of seeing the God in things. As technological innovation led to exploration and expansion, so, too, did the world expand at the personal level. Passion for God's creations—be it bird or bloom—was exalted.

Later, botany would become more formalized as plant hunters set off around the globe, and botanical art would reach its zenith. But during the Baroque, we have the great floral painters and engravers, who offer a glimpse of the varieties of flowers popular at the time.

For Dutch flowers, see Rachel Ruysch (1664–1750), a prolific painter who had access to new varieties of flowers through her father, a professor of botany, and later through her own success. (It has been said that she made more money for a flower painting than Rembrandt did for a portrait.) Jan van Huysum (1662–1749) lived in Amsterdam but traveled to the gardens of Haarlem to sketch new varieties of flowers, which he would later incorporate into his still life work. (His sketches and watercolors are particularly fine, though his oils are legendary.) For French inspiration from the period, look to the engravings of Jean-Baptiste Monnoyer (1636–1699) in *Le Livre de toutes sortes de fleurs d'après nature* (The book of all kinds of flowers from nature). In England the nurseryman Robert Furber (1674–1756) produced a series of engravings as a quasi seed catalogue titled *Twelve Months of Flowers* in 1730, which provides an interesting record of over four hundred seasonal flowers (and reveals the Georgian fetish for breeding specialty auriculas).

TEN THINGS TO LEARN FROM THE BAROQUE

The Baroque was a period of radical transformation. Here are a few ideas drawn from Baroque music, art, and architecture.

1. Use gesture and movement to initiate emotional response. Make people feel something when they look at your work.
2. Indulge in complexity and embellishment, but resist chaos.
3. When photographing your flowers, use a light source that is dramatic but ambiguous, outside the image itself.
4. Make people feel as if they are in the same space as the flowers you photograph. In painting, this is referred to as "open form," which means the viewer has a sense that the full story cannot be contained by the image and thus it opens beyond itself.
5. Develop contrast and volume through the manipulation of light and dark. Remember chiaroscuro.
6. Observation of the natural world and the materiality of things can lead to great art.
7. Draped and rippled fabric and ribbons allow you to play with light and show off your artistic prowess.
8. In Baroque music, there's a sense of abandon but also of control, created through the repetition of motif and rhythm. In Baroque gardens, such as those at Het Loo in the Netherlands or Hampton Court in England, grandeur is always tempered with restraint.
9. Use rich colors and dark backgrounds to tell the truth about human suffering and passion.
10. Recognize that history informs your work. Just as the Baroque painters looked to the classical world for education and inspiration, know that you, too, have been sculpted in your aesthetics and understanding of beauty.

# The Dutch Masters

*[Still life] is an art that points to the human by leaving the human out;*
*nowhere visible, we're everywhere. It is an art that points to meaning through*
*wordlessness, that points to timelessness through things permanently caught in*
*time....*

*And perhaps that's another of the paintings' secrets: they satisfy so deeply*
*because they offer us intimacy and distance at once, allow us both to be here*
*and gone.*

—MARK DOTY

## STILL LIFE

In the seventeenth century, Dutch art and culture blossomed into what is now known as the Dutch Golden Age. Ships under the direction of the Dutch East India Company brought exotic plants and spices to the Netherlands, and trade in everything from pepper to coffee to sugar fueled tremendous economic growth. The population of Amsterdam leapt from thirty thousand to two hundred thousand in the latter part of the century as trade increased. A merchant class emerged, and the purchase of art, once possible for only a few, came into fashion. Small, easel-sized *stilleven*, or still life paintings, became popular as a means to brighten homes.

Some have argued that early Dutch flower paintings served as a record of new varieties and species, while others have suggested the works served as status markers, providing the new merchants with vehicles for investment. Whatever the reason for their proliferation, for two hundred years Netherlandish still life elevated everyday beauty into works of great art, and floral designers have forever been grateful.

Early Dutch flower paintings featured a selection of blooms arranged symmetrically and a bit stiffly, each painted in exquisite detail and illuminated by even, impartial light. At this time, around 1600 to 1650, the flowers often were depicted in a niche, with little depth to the arrangement. A hierarchy of flowers prevailed, with the "holy" flowers, such as *Fritillaria imperialis*—itself an import from the Ottoman Empire—or lilies (representing the purity of the Virgin Mary), appearing above the "noble" flowers, such as roses and dianthus. Wildflowers usually appeared lower in the piece, and a few objects such as shells might be arranged below the flowers for a kind of object lesson in the Great Chain of Being.

Floral still lifes weren't painted directly from life but rather from studies of individual plants, arranged only on the canvas. This is one of the reasons why flowers with different bloom times appear together, such as spring hyacinths with summer roses—and why Dutch Masters' arrangements are hard to replicate in purely seasonal floral designs. It also wasn't uncommon for the same arc of a special tulip to appear in multiple paintings. (Speaking of tulips, I must digress: The tulip first traveled from Turkey to Vienna in 1554, making landfall in the Netherlands in 1578, where, according to the British anthropologist Jack Goody, "the soil proved especially suitable." The result was the Dutch bulb trade and the boom/bust of tulipomania—the crazed climate surrounding a flower so valuable it was traded as currency.)

By the mid-seventeenth century, the style of Dutch floral still life had become more animated, looser, with the backs of some petals turned to the viewer and more space around the stems. Consider the bold, flowing polychromatic paintings of Rachel Ruysch, wherein flowers are set against a dark background, each petal rendered with the meticulous detail of a miniaturist, each insect alive on its legs.

Later still, in the eighteenth century, the paintings grew fuller, with blown flowers and fruits. Accessories were grouped at the base of arrangements; in the work of Jan van Huysum, sweeping S-curves created dramatic movement, the frame practically spilling with abundance and extravagance.

Given these stylistic differences, then, what precisely is a Dutch Masters–style arrangement in floral design? I'd argue a simulacrum, an approximation, a work of art inspired by art.

I've long loved the images of the contemporary American photographer Sharon Core, who explores still life and the boundaries between truth and illusion. For a number of years she re-created the florals of famous painters—Odilon Redon, Charles Willson Peale, and the Dutch Masters—playing with our visual memory of great works. As the poet Donna Stonecipher once posited, Core's work forces us to consider, "How many 'lives' does a still life have?"

But before we swerve fully into the present, let's consider the plants and flowers so important to this history of Dutch art. Our economy doesn't take long to deliver on desire—drones will soon drop flower bulbs at our doors. But consider your own lust for blooms when you look at these works of art. You may wait a year or two to obtain the corm of a freshly bred butterfly ranunculus from a Dutch grower, but it's not as if you had to spend weeks at sea to first touch one. Similarly, in a world saturated with images, it's difficult to imagine the wonder and thrill of seeing a new species of flower for the first time or the magic of its rendering by an artist.

In the two-hundred-year span of these paintings, botany developed as separate from medicine and ornamental floriculture spread across Europe. The Dutch Golden Age not only created great art but also helped to make the Netherlands the horticultural powerhouse it is today.

## KUNST- UND WUNDERKAMMERN

As ships offloaded exotic finds into European ports in the seventeenth century, collectors amassed treasures from foreign lands. These marvels (and the Baroque was the age of the marvel) might be kept in *Kunst- und Wunderkammern*, a German term for a cabinet of curiosities, a room or space that came into vogue in the Renaissance and persisted for hundreds of years as the precursor to the museum. Designed to offer analysis and amazement, these collections were also vehicles to display wealth and status.

Such "curious" objects as well as more mundane items held metaphorical meaning in Dutch still life painting. A caterpillar nibbling a leaf was both a nod to creation and a powerful reminder of the transient nature of life itself. These *memento mori* (which roughly translates from the Latin as "remember that you have to die") served to moralize in the Dutch Calvinist tradition. Referred to also as *vanitas* (Latin for "vanity"), they reminded the viewer of the sin of indulging in the pleasures of the senses and served as a kind of cultural commentary on Dutch acquisitiveness.

Developing your own cabinet of curiosities can be helpful for still life work. While this list relates to the symbolism of the Dutch Masters, there's really no limit these days to what can be used for symbolic purposes with flowers—crunched plastic bottles, polyester netting, you name it—but if you're going for the Golden Age, try these (adapted from the "Guide to Period Flower Arranging" by the National Association of Flower Arranging Societies of Great Britain):

**Earthly existence:** books, pearls, jewelry, goblets, seashells, musical instruments, knives

**Transience of life:** holes in leaves and the insects or reptiles that ate them; skulls; hourglasses and clocks; lit candles; peeled and marred fruit, such as cherries, oranges, plums, apricots, grapes, and melons

**Resurrection:** birds' nests with eggs, butterflies, ivies, ears of corn

**Other:** Stuffed birds, mushrooms, chestnuts (both in their cases and out), gemstones and crystals, pewter plates, copper vessels, Delftware, glistening whole fish, oysters on the half shell, lemon peel, pineapple (popular in the eighteenth century), currants (the white variety are particularly luminescent)

**Tip:** To add shine to fruit, paint it with a little olive oil. You can use a spray bottle for misting flowers to create dew and droplets, but a pressurized product like Caudalie grape water is easier to work with. Museum wax, bamboo skewers, mounting pins, and straight pins are also helpful for positioning objects and insects. Keep textiles like Persian carpets, lace, and linen handy for draping and concealing.

TEN THINGS TO LEARN FROM DUTCH FLORAL STILL LIFE
Dutch flower pieces are one of many forms of still life paintings produced during the Dutch Golden Age, circa 1600–1800. While they altered in style over that time, most are not representations of actual floral arrangements, but studies of individual flowers masterfully assembled on the canvas. That said, much can be learned from the paintings. Consider:

1. Beauty is transient. Honor change and decay.
2. Don't be afraid of using primary colors (together).
3. Cover the lip of your vase.
4. Branches and stems can lead the eye from one flower to the next.
5. Show off individual flowers. Capture a sense of wonder.
6. Asymmetry is a stylistic choice, not an obligation.
7. Develop a depth wish. Create layers of interest in your arrangement and floral photographs.
8. Remember your frame, be that the wall you are planning to position your arrangement against or the frame of the photograph you plan to take.
9. Use memento mori to create visual interest (if not teach lessons).
10. Arranging groups of objects requires patience and a keen eye. Try not to underestimate the skill and time that goes into styling.

# Rococo Style

The decorative style known as Rococo arose in France after the death of Louis XIV, marking a departure from the formality of the Baroque. Nobles set up smaller residences away from the demands of the court, decorating them in pastel colors reflecting the levity of the age.

Like the Baroque, French Rococo decorative style favored complex forms and intricate details, but there was a greater interest in fragility, intimacy, and playfulness. Natural motifs such as waves, shells, dolphins, leaves, fruit, and flowers were carved into furniture, embroidered on light-colored silks, and painted on porcelain. Grace and beauty reigned.

The term *Rococo* comes from the French *rocaille* (rock) and *coquille* (shell). The colors of the period? Shell pink, abalone, pale and golden yellows, watery hyacinth and larkspur blues, turquoise, and pearlescent grays. And of course, gold—gilding in particular.

One ubiquitous design motif was the crest of a wave. In floral design, movement and asymmetry dominated, but, as with the Baroque, the emphasis was always on elegance. Very little foliage was used in Rococo floral design in order to highlight the beauty (and often the scent) of the flowers. The leaves of flowers might be incorporated into a design or a trailing vine added for gesture, but floriferous is an apt description of Rococo floral style. Popular flowers included roses—namely, *R. centifolia, damascena,* and *gallica*—poppies, lilies, anemones, tulips, primulas, hollyhocks, honeysuckles, clematises, cornflowers, irises, dianthus, and *Fritillaria imperialis*.

The still life paintings of the Dutch artist Gerard van Spaendonck are illustrative of Rococo floral style, as are those by Anne Vallayer-Coster, who served as painter in the court of Marie Antoinette.

Strong contrast was avoided, with the exception of the dramatic use of light in gardens and their portrayal in art—mystery hinted at passion. The painters François Boucher and Jean-Antoine Watteau might depict classical sculpture from the Baroque overtaken by lush foliage, roses cascading over walls, and nature as a place of fecundity, love, and idyllic tranquility. In France, this was the era for romantic assignations in gardens or grottos and time spent in nature at *fêtes galantes*.

The Rococo also brought new ideas about society to the fore. Salons became fashionable as Madame de Pompadour played hostess to *philosophes*, and in Paris, cafes provided new opportunities for the mixing of classes. Discussion of social issues and democracy emerged in France, and in England debates about aesthetics developed. The picturesque landscape—rugged, rustic, varied—became fashionable.

A romantic ensemble of *Rosa banksiae* 'Lutea' made with Beth Parrott

# How to Build a Pouf

In 1775 Marie Antoinette had her hair styled atop her head for her husband's coronation. The look created a sensation. Her upswept hair, powdered and decorated with feathers and jewels, screamed opulence and signaled power.

The pouf is still with us today. From desserts to flowers, lofty, elaborate confections are always built upon a structure. In the late eighteenth century, women wore metal frames on top of their heads and used light pillows to support the hair. Similarly, building a "tower of power" without floral foam requires thought about volume and weight, but the guiding principle of the style hasn't changed much in over two hundred years—more is always more.

A parallel lesson: At the dawn of the nineteenth century, a grand dessert was invented—the croquembouche. Loosely translated from the French as "crunch in the mouth," a croquembouche is a cone-shaped confection made of small choux pastry puffs filled with whipped cream and bound together with caramelized sugar.

Honestly, it's divine.

My son didn't like cloying cakes and icing as a child, so come birthdays, I went for the pouf. I sometimes built the thing over a wine bottle—this is cheating, of course, but a solid structure is key in the initial stages.

Which brings me back to flowers. If you need to make something higher than your stems' lengths can go, cover and fill a wire frame with wet moss to tuck your stems into or buy some thin, green florist's wire and invest in some reusable plastic tubes. You may have seen these on single-stem roses. Easily found online and usually made of clear plastic, they have nifty flexible collars that accommodate varying stem circumferences. You can feed these into a chicken wire frame, or use water receptacles (funnel vases or plastic bottles), zip-tying or wiring them in. Be sure your wire base is secured. Towers have a tendency to tip, and though it has never happened to me while singing "Happy Birthday," I've made certain I've only had to carry my creations a short distance. As Marie Antoinette learned, over-the-top style can have dire consequences.

# Hogarth's Line of Beauty

*Nature abhors a straight line.*

—WILLIAM KENT

In the summer of 2018, I was invited to teach the florists of Chatsworth House in Derbyshire, England. The honor was immense—the Duke of Devonshire's florists? me? how?—but what was far larger than my impostor syndrome was the estate itself. At thirty-five thousand acres, the estate contains farms, houses, multiple gardens, forested land, and, most famously, around Chatsworth House itself, a vast park designed by Lancelot "Capability" Brown.

In the eighteenth century, the idea of the pastoral idyll was in vogue among the English aristocracy. What might such an idyll have looked like? I found out the minute I drove in: hummocky hills (which Brown had shaped) rippled into a valley dotted with clumps of broadleaf trees. Sheep nibbled the grass, looking like figurines placed about for effect. After a few minutes, the scale of the landscaping baffled me. When the house came into view, I felt (as was intended by the designer) as if I had slipped inside a picturesque painting.

I'd done some cursory homework beforehand: I'd watched a BBC series about Chatsworth and read a slim book about Capability Brown on my train ride to Derbyshire, so I'd expected to be impressed, but the thing one forgets about impressions is the pressure part. The house pressed upon me. Its grandeur, its history, its art.

And I was expected to create some myself the following day.

On my arrival, I was toured about the gardens to scout for plants to use in my design and meet the staff. Later, I wandered alone through the public portions of the house (the duke and duchess still live in a portion of it), past towering tulipieres, old still lifes, and sculptures that swayed, posed, and

*Lilium regale* with opalescent pink petals and bright yellow anthers served as the color cornerstone for this arrangement at Chatsworth House in England. Also pictured: *Rosa* 'Felicia', *Eryngium* 'Miss Wilmott's Ghost', dahlias, fennel, and astilbes. The foliage here is olive and *Plectranthus argentatus*. Thanks to Zara Reid, Becky Crowley, and the intrepid Chatsworth team for holding up this sheet of plastic for the photo.

roared. The Cavendish family has collected art for generations, so fixing a period for the style of my arrangement I found challenging. Narrow my options—yes, but how?

I was visiting in early July, which meant the delphiniums were perfect, the roses sublime, and a vast array of flowers, grown by Becky Crowley and her team in the cutting garden, were on offer. I could pick anything and everything, but to do so would show a lack of restraint and professionalism. I had to choose a palette, but which one?

It's always best to lead with one flower that calls to you, one flower at the height of perfection, and for me that day, the regal lilies called. White with brilliant yellow stamens, the lilies would lead my design, of that I became sure. The backs of their petals shade from dusky gray to pink. My next issue: a vessel that might support them.

The head florist, Zara Reid, showed me the choices available. I'd been hoping for something magnificent, if not gold, but opulent artifacts were sadly not on offer, so we dug around in a dusty old shed and found an urn big enough to accommodate the tall lilies.

With two fundamentals established, I felt more confident. I was driven to a nearby inn (the duke's), where I ate some of his lovely estate lamb and thought about my day. Lilies, so loaded with religious meaning, were popular in the Renaissance and through the Baroque. The urn was a classical replica, but I had miles to go on dating urns, so…stick with what you know. And what did I know? The Rococo.

Blame my love of peace and adornment, how I swoon for gilt, silk, yellow, lightness, and parties. The Rococo makes me feel as if I'd have been very good at being a rich Parisienne, having a salon, bantering with bubbly in hand, taking lovers…forgetting the crippling corsets and powder-haired men, of course.

But where was I?

The next morning, picking from the garden.

Having a narrative to unfurl while you teach is half of the showmanship, so I spun a tale as I worked involving the flowers growing on-site and the historical influences that had shaped the landscape around the house.

I opted for mid- to late eighteenth-century naturalism as expressed during the Rococo (this was also the Georgian period in England, but more on that later). As mentioned, the Rococo is associated with levity and frivolity in the decorative arts (not to mention a surfeit of scrolls and waves), and with a squint, one could say the glow of the lilies' petals resembled the pearly quality of shells.

Of course, some creative license is always at play (and play was de rigueur after the formality and heavy colors of the Baroque), but I think it's useful and fun to provide artistic work with a context, a sensibility—not only to guide one's practice but to give us all a language with which to interpret our work and to give floral design the artistic heft it deserves.

So: my colors were intentionally opalescent, led by the lilies and roses that were popular in the age. In the late eighteenth century—the Georgian "age of elegance" in England—pale greens and blues came into favor, so the *Plectranthus* and *Eryngium* 'Miss Wilmott's Ghost' reflect that luminosity.

The form I chose was based on the English artist William Hogarth's "line of beauty": the serpentine line was common for loose floriferous arrangements of the time. Hogarth gave his 1753 theoretical treatise *The Analysis of Beauty* the subtitle "Written with a view of fixing the fluctuating IDEAS of TASTE." Interestingly, he also poked fun at the whimsical picturesque gardens of William Kent, who opened the way for the idylls of Capability Brown—for me, layers on layers of inspiration.

At last, after I photographed the arrangement (that's a black plastic sheet behind the urn, held aloft by two game Chatsworth florists; see page 153), it was moved to Flora's Temple, which itself had been moved alongside the house in 1750, just a few years before Hogarth shared his ideas.

PART SIX

# DESIGNING

# On Creativity

*A flower...is never just...a flower, but a resource for the exploration of color possibilities, of the evanescence of light and movement, the study of form and structure.*

—PENELOPE LIVELY

Often I have people say to me, "Oh, you're so creative," as if it were an attribute I was born with. Nature or nurture? In my case, neither, I suspect.

I know my parents did a few seventies things right: left me to dance with headphones on, encouraged play outdoors, and gave me artistic license to paint murals in my room. But no one in my family was a dedicated designer, writer, or artist, and I wouldn't have had a clue how to become one, even if I'd believed I could. (And that believing, that sense of confidence to step on the path—that knowledge that the path even exists and where it may lead—is significant.)

Creatives, in my opinion, are largely made, not born. For me, the term *creative discipline* means just that: you show up, you do the work. You put your butt in the chair or your eyes on the vase or camera, and you educate yourself. Perhaps this is what Constance Spry meant when she said of floristry: "An eye can be trained more readily than a character changed." Temperament may have more to do with talent than we think.

Training and practice help one to develop artistically. That needn't be heavy or limiting, but it is work, and some days it feels like it to me: the well is dry, ideas used up. But if you cultivate creativity, it does grow. You just have to give it your attention.

If you're busy, you might drop a flower in a vase in passing and simply spend a few minutes positioning it just right or keep an arrangement in progress as you set about chores. I often see a flower in its prime and know I should use it, if not quite how or for whom. Occasionally I'll work on two or three orders at once over a few hours, playing among them. That luxury of the time to stretch out the process of creation? For me, it's harder to achieve than the work itself.

So give yourself a day. Give yourself an hour. Give yourself time to learn.

I once listened to an interview with the Booker Prize–winning novelist and poet Michael Ondaatje while I was processing flowers for a design. The interviewer leaned on him, saying that after reading the first few pages, he wasn't sure what direction Ondaatje's new novel would take.

Ondaatje replied, "I'm one of those writers who actually doesn't know what's going to happen when I begin a book.…[I] kind of begin with a situation, and then gradually a story will form."

I looked down at the buckets of flowers at my feet and agreed. My situation? Too much of a good thing. But it made me think of the perennial question of any design: Where to begin?

In the garden or the flower shop, the spark for a design is often prompted by a feeling of astonishment. Something new blooms or arrives, and you simply must have a closer look. Or you're obsessing about your napkin color for a party (it has happened to the best of us) and see just the right shade of flower. You forget the tableau of buckets before you or your border of blooms because that singular flower is what has caught you up and holds you. So there you begin.

Ondaatje went on to paraphrase the jazz musician Ornette Coleman: "The thing you play at the beginning is a territory; what follows is the adventure."

Indeed: that first branch or flower you play is the note that resonates throughout the work. But bear with me because I have a digression and lesson about the adventure–the middle of the work–that requires a guilty admission: I've become hooked on listening to podcasts while I work. Quite literally, too: I tuck my phone in a back pocket or my bra–anything to stay plugged in. Hence, the Ondaatje.

But what do we lose when we forsake silence while we work?

Flow, apparently. *Flow*, in psychological terms, refers to an optimal experience, a time when we feel a kind of deep involvement with an activity. My husband surfs or skis his way there, and many of us weed or paint or design our way there, though *there* may not be the right term because flow is fluid, a kind of easy dancing of consciousness when thoughts come and go and we feel at peace. Many people experience the feeling with or in nature. You feel comfortable in silence, your mind unspooling, your senses firing and body working as you relax into a deeper awareness.

For me, the middle of a design is a period of flow. I work intuitively, not fretting too much about rules or color. I just keep my hands moving and senses engaged.

Of course, real limitations apply to working with flowers: a stuffed vase, a wilting leaf, time itself. You want me to achieve flow under such constraints? you may ask. Yes, I do, if only for a short time, because that's when the magic happens, when an idea might find expression free of thought.

So try to give yourself over to the flowers in silence. In Japanese ikebana, it's accepted that what is within the designer will come to light through the arranging of plants. You probably want to be witness to that, like it or not.

I've noticed that the muddling middle is where perfectionists struggle most. They push hard and overthink, and the work pushes back. It will not behave. What to do?

"If you set aside confidence in your capacity, if you release your weight into the graceful engine of something other than your will, you may find yourself coming alongside things," says the environmental poet Tim Lilburn. "If desire begins to act as an ascetic power, an emptying force at odds with the aplomb of the self, then . . . you may arrive."

Humility and a reverence for nature help you get through.

If that fails, treat your arrangement like a temperamental beast and turn your back on it. See how it survives on its own.

Later, check in: Can you feel a pulse? What are its vitals?

I think of this return as a period of analysis; with fresh eyes, we can decipher the work. What have you done? You may have cut stems so short they cannot be made longer, but they can be moved, the work tweaked. You can go read a few of the writer Joan D. Stamm's tenets of ikebana ("Don't go against a plant's natural growth. Each flower, like each person, should shine with individual uniqueness.")

If your work is tight, you can stick your fingers into your arrangement like you might someone's hair and rustle it up to loosen it. If it still feels stiff, you can bang the whole affair on a table to make it relax (obviously not Zen, but it can work with maximalist designs).

"You start a painting," Picasso once said, "and it becomes something altogether different. It's strange how little the artist's will matters."

Often we need to succumb to succeed.

# On Style

*The truly fashionable are beyond fashion.*

—CECIL BEATON

## WHAT IS STYLE?

In floral design or garden design, we might recognize a designer's work by a particular plant palette they use or by the manner in which they approach space. Some floral designers go low and stay there—stems more horizontal than vertical, with empty space central to the arrangement, much the way in which some garden designers might envision a path through a meadow before they outline its edge.

A person's approach to color might signal style—a love of bold or warm colors or the use of complementaries or analogous schemes. But these are all elements of style, one could say, not the ineffable thing itself.

The irony (or ecstasy) for me of this book's subtitle, *The Elements of Floral Style,* is that I once taught an undergraduate course titled singularly and just as ominously Elements of Style. This was in a creative writing department. I was recently out of grad school, and I suspect no senior professor wanted to take it on. The course mixed poets with journalists—not an easy crowd, but everyone had the same materials to work with, at least: words.

I began the course with the galling "What is style?" question. And, failing to have an answer, I trotted out a bunch of quotes by luminaries instead:

> *The style is the man.*
>
> —ROBERT FROST

> *Style…is a relationship, the relation in art between form and content.*
>
> —CYRIL CONNOLLY

Had I been teaching fashion design instead of writing, similar pithy bits might have been tossed about; I suspect they helped no one, at least not those young people just beginning to strive for their own style.

So I sashayed around the topic of style and taught rhythm and punctuation and syntax instead. I taught the elements of style without answering the question itself.

When I teach floral design workshops, I again break down style—to color, to texture, to shape, and to space. We all need a language for interpreting our work in order to learn. And I believe everyone can develop a style and—with even more effort—change theirs.

Monet moved toward abstraction over time and van Gogh toward bold colors. But if those two are any example, it takes immense amounts of work: Monet produced about 2,500 paintings and van Gogh in his short life produced about 2,000 works of art. Picasso shifted styles a number of times and left over 50,000 sketches, drawings, sculptures, and paintings to prove it.

I often feel frustrated when an arrangement looks like I made it, because I want to surprise myself and too rarely do. Throughout my apprenticeship with flowers, I have avoided developing a style and failed by acquiring one. (I'm not sure why precisely I didn't want one—perhaps I have no interest in being a brand or the idea of a style felt like a cage.)

So I've tried to borrow styles and to adapt them to the flowers I have on hand. In retrospect, I think this is a sensible process for the neophyte: study, copy, flounder, and, by necessity, invent. Having access to new blooms helps; like new colors in a paint box, they challenge you to see differently. A change of scene or venue also scrapes away old habits.

To borrow from the writer Howard Jacobson, in the hot pursuit of style we should set out to discover rather than assert. We should go places we never expected to go and get lost along the way.

Art, as Jacobson notes, must constantly "test its flights of abstraction against…obstinate materiality." At the altar of style, thankfully, flowers will always push us humbly down to earth.

# Pentimento

As I work a design, I often think of the term *pentimento*, from the Italian verb *pentirsi*, which means "to repent." In painting, pentimento refers to a change made by the artist in the process of painting. This could be at the level of the underpainting or a later alteration, a layer of paint telling the story of a change of heart.

How often do we do this as we assemble flowers in a vase? We begin in one direction and take off in another. Vestiges of early decisions linger—a base note of foliage, say, or a flower reversed from view or an over-trimmed branch tucked under a flower as a prop. Much as in painting, these are traces of previous decisions, hidden beneath the surface of the work but still a fundamental part of it.

This July arrangement began with coppery ninebark foliage, then progressed to the burgundy and cream umbels of *Daucus carota* 'Dara', then tufts of thalictrum, Shirley poppies, and finally 'Suzy Z' and 'Crimson Ripple' sweet peas for filler. The ninebark is there, but barely visible, as its color proved too warm to move forward in the arrangement, yet it still supports the piece's backside and adds depth to the work.

To borrow from the painter Sanya Kantarovsky, we can find meaning and pleasure in "revealing the doing in the done." All artists change their mind.

# Restraint and Constraint

*How do you exercise the restraint that simplicity requires without crossing over
into ostentatious austerity? How do you pay attention to all the necessary details
without becoming excessively fussy? How do you achieve simplicity without
inviting boredom?... Pare down the essence, but don't remove the poetry.*
—LEONARD KOREN

## ON RESTRAINT

I pass a house on my walk that beguiles me with its perfection. The house
is from the 1930s, stucco and painted in gray, white, and black. The effect:
contrast, so your eye moves from the black roof to the gray walls to the
black shutters and the white of the window trim. The white makes the
house look awake. The foggy gray is there but not there: a precisely chosen
backdrop to the flowers planted every spring in window boxes and on the
steps—brilliant red geraniums. Forgive this voguish verb: the flowers pop.
You can't help but see them. All those cool tones irrevocably draw you to
the warmth of the red.

On the avenue in front of the house, the owner again shows restraint.
Set against a trim yew hedge, huddled under a birch and surrounded by
fresh dark compost, is a ring of crisp, white New Guinea impatiens. The
implication is control. The effect is precision. And I admire it because I
lack such restraint.

My garden is a collection of affections—plants I love singly and
en masse. Flowers raised from seed or rescued from a neighbor's garden, plants inherited, purchased, or acquired at great effort and expense
through sheer determination. You could say I run an orphanage or a tiny
farm. Restraint, when it comes to flowers, I lack.

I knew I needed to learn how to do more with less. So my own maximalist twelve-step program began at my local senior center, in a class led by
Fumi Csizmazia, who had studied ikebana as a part of nursing training in
Japan. Ikebana in various forms has been practiced in Asia since the sixth
century. Csizmazia emphasized the therapeutic and meditative aspects of
the art, teaching us to listen to the materials while finding a means of creative expression.

We began each session with finger exercises and stretches. We consciously breathed. Then Csizmazia explained how in ikebana both the maker and the viewer should be reminded that nothing is perfect. Each display should signify emotion, season, and circumstance.

Csizmazia had three tips to guide the arranging process—what she calls her "CBA list," which emphasizes the importance of believing in yourself and also of stepping outside yourself and bowing down before beauty:

C:  Concentrate on the hidden beauty of the material you are working with;

B:  Be aware of your unique creativity;

A:  Appreciate the created form, which does not exist in nature's setting.

The angle and height of each branch in many styles of ikebana is set, prescribed. I struggled with the rules but also paradoxically felt safe within them. I came to see how making choices becomes easier within constraints.

## ON CONSTRAINT

Constraint provides us with useful limits. Constraint makes boundaries clear. Constraint tightens our focus so we can better see the work ahead and avoid wallowing in limitless options.

Your vessel or your access to flowers may serve as a constraint. Budgets constrain our choices, forcing us to do more with less. And time is almost always a constraint. But there's another type of constraint that niggles at me—one tied to the history of women and plants.

Throughout history, flowers have provided women with a means of expression. Whether we're talking about the ancient art of ikebana or the language of flowers in Victorian England, flowers have served as communication tools for women who have lacked a voice in patriarchal cultures. A posy, a tussie-mussie, or a petite work of art in a teahouse might have served as a tool for subterfuge and resistance. Women have long found agency by speaking through flowers.

European and colonial women in the eighteenth and nineteenth centuries were not permitted formal study, but they were supported in the "soft"

In Victorian times, strident colors swept into fashion as a result of the new aniline dyes the Industrial Revolution produced: mauvine, violets, puce, magenta, mulberry, mustard, and carnation pink. In everything from the carpet bedding style of hothouse-grown plants from Africa and South America to the chemically dyed fabrics of the period, Victorian fashion embraced the new.

Here I've used late-season perennials in bloom at the Cambo Estate, taking my color cue from the Victorian period, when the house was built. The real star here is the *Rodgersia*, both its tall, rusty, plume-shaped flowers and yellowing palmate leaves. And yes, that's a copper pot, which I daresay would not have been used for flower arranging by ladies once upon a time, but it was fantastically flat for resting on my shoulder while I roamed and hefted, chasing the light for a photograph.

sciences. Botany became all the rage. According to the writer Jennifer Bennett, botany meant "a woman could, without losing her grasp of the Victorian notion of fragile femininity, take a greater part in the world."

Collecting plants meant roaming outdoors, away from the strictures of the house, and offered liberation from domestic roles and duties. Identifying foraged flowers and plants, painting them, pressing them, skeletonizing them, and arranging them became sanctioned indoor pursuits.

In the Victorian period, women were not only named for (and compared to) flowers but also directly spoke through them. Feelings, thoughts, and attitudes could be conveyed through a bouquet. As Lina Krasnovaitė observes, the rituals were complex:

> Everything had symbolic meaning: the way a bouquet was given, the way it was received and held....Victorians used bouquets to denote not only sympathy, friendship or love, but also negative attitude or even insult.

This language of flowers, as scholar Anna Svensson notes, "was highly performative...and required precise knowledge of and adherence to the rules, because it was a language designed to communicate emotional states between people."

That makes the practice sound quaint, but the counterpoint (of which Svensson is aware) is that the language of flowers was loaded with cultural baggage: Orientalism, Christianity, occultism, and sexism. I can't unpack all that here (Jack Goody makes an ethnobotanical attempt in *The Culture of Flowers*), but suffice it to say there were also positives that arose from the fad: the language of flowers led to a kind of democratization of flowers and helped fuel floral passions in the art and poetry of the period.

The Japanese version of the language of flowers is called *hanakotoba*. In ikebana, a style of flower arranging that means, loosely, "giving life to flowers," a range of meanings is similarly expressed through plants. Ikebana is grounded in polytheistic animism, wherein spirit resides in all things—a bud, a stone, a branch, a tuft of moss—so that the art of ikebana, despite its apparent spareness, speaks volumes.

## TEN THINGS TO LEARN FROM IKEBANA

An ancient tradition, ikebana has many different styles. Here are some basic principles to help inform your designs.

1. Cut sparingly and with compassion for the plants.
2. Your display should signify the season.
3. Your vessel is not a holder but an integral part of your design.
4. Don't arrange flowers you don't know the names of. It shows a lack of respect for the plants.
5. Try to highlight overlooked forms of beauty.
6. Space is not meant to be filled but created. The three elements of ikebana are line, color, and mass.
7. Form is found, not planned.
8. The meditative aspect of floral arranging has a therapeutic effect. Silence will bring you closer to nature.
9. Floral symbolism matters in many cultural traditions. Ensure your blooms suit the occasion and will not offend.
10. Consider the setting for your arrangement.

← From left: *Ribes* 'White Icicle', *Anemone* 'Galilee Albino', *Helleborus* 'Double Ellen', *Leucojum aestivum, Helleborus argutifolius, Narcissus* 'Tete-a-Tete' and *Fritillaria raddeana.*

# Wabi Sabi

From the insect-eaten leaf in classical still life to the wilting bloom or blown petals of a flower, symbols of transience can be used to elevate floral art. Flowers, whether in bud, bloom, or decay, are vulnerable to weather, pests, human contact, and time. Ephemeral and often exquisitely imperfect, flowers connect us to natural processes.

The Japanese concept of *wabi sabi* speaks to this understanding. As Leonard Koren writes in his classic *Wabi-Sabi for Artists, Designers, Poets and Philosophers,* "Wabi sabi is a beauty of things imperfect, impermanent, and incomplete. It is a beauty of things modest and humble. It is a beauty of things unconventional."

When one thinks about *wabi sabi*, the aesthetic principles of Zen philosophy are useful to keep in mind. These include:

**Kanso:** *simplicity*

**Fukinsei:** *asymmetry or irregularity*

**Shibumi:** *beauty of the understated*

**Shizen:** *naturalness without pretense*

**Yugen:** *subtle grace*

**Datsuzoku:** *freeness*

**Seijaku:** *tranquility*

In this image of a leaky, tipping old vessel, I'm heartily reminded of imperfection. The surface of the vessel is worn and flaking, which resonates with wabi sabi ideas, and though I can't rightly say that the arrangement of seasonal flowers is wabi sabi, given all its color and busyness, the humble bracken arching out at right manifests wabi sabi ideas of the earthy and unconventional. (I made the piece to showcase the spiky eremurus—an act of hauteur entirely—but the bracken helps ground the work.) To borrow from Koren again, wabi sabi "is comfortable with ambiguity and contradiction," and I'm comfortable with this result of muddled intentions. (Imperfection is similarly embraced in the Japanese practice of *kintsugi,* which involves making visible repairs to a piece of pottery to showcase the beauty of its age. Perhaps that's next for this vessel.)

An autumn leaf falling from a branch indoors, a display of pine cones in a chipped bowl, an arrangement of buds set to bloom—these are wabi sabi, perchance. It depends on your approach, so check your motives. As Koren says, "The simplicity of wabi sabi is best described as the state of grace arrived at by a sober, modest, heartfelt intelligence." That can't be achieved overnight.

# DEEPENING
# YOUR WORK

# Why Floral Design?

Floral design is both an art and a craft. But do I call myself an "artist" or a "craftsperson"—or dodge that binary entirely and use the word *designer*?

I don't know.

When I was stewing about the place of floral design in the world (and my place in it), my friend Aniela Woodward wrote me this:

> Floral arrangement has historically been considered a decorative art, along with interior design, carpets, mosaics, etc.
>
> What is the function of a floral arrangement? To beautify, to enhance, to decorate, to create a visual effect. Fine art, on the other hand, may have an intellectual agenda and historically has had permanence that allowed time for contemplation. So today we can still see sculptures by Michelangelo or the paintings by Titian or the floral still lifes of the Dutch.
>
> Today, contemporary floral arrangements gain permanency through photography, and as a result, all the old criteria of Fine Art vs. Decorative is blurred.

I felt somewhat better after reading this but also considered that a number of floral and environmental artists today build installations that are meant to be experienced rather than photographed. They may be political, too. Contemplation ensues, analysis abounds—we immerse ourselves in flowers and see the world in a new way.

In this section I offer advice on developing your work, with the caveat that I am in the middle of a flowery journey myself. Whether you move toward the fine arts through creating photographs and installations or toward craftsmanship through developing a design business or come up with another means of sharing flowers with others, let me add one more tidbit to bolster the creative in you: floral design has long transgressed boundaries—between outdoor space and domestic space, between the cultural and the natural, and between art and craft.

There is so much uncharted territory open to us. As my historian friend Lise Butler once said to me, "Wherever a gap exists is interesting."

Go there.

Learning about floral design by watching someone create a piece in front of you is heady stuff; as you witness the process of creation, you learn how another person sees. Online tutorials exist, but nothing beats a live performance for an honest display of both professional talent and the second-guessing that often accompanies it.

In the remainder of the book, I address the question "Now what?" What if you love flowers, have grown some or procured some, and feel like you're getting the knack of arranging them? You might want to pursue something—be it as small as a printed photograph or as large as a small business—but don't know where to begin.

Take heart: there are plenty who can teach you the skills. Workshops in floral design are offered both through professional associations and to the public in a range of venues—everything from an evening centerpiece class to a destination workshop in a grand old country house. Classes in flower farming, bouquet making, the business of floristry, floral photography, still life composition, or a blend of all of the above (and more) are available throughout the world. Pop a hashtag before any of those words or phrases on Instagram and you'll see a wide selection online—or ask a designer you're fond of if they teach.

Professional floristry is taught at community colleges, floristry schools, and design institutions. Certification varies by country, but the program of study usually covers the care and handling of fresh flowers, concepts in floral design, wedding work, event planning, installation work, business practices, and so on. Seek out an accredited school if you are contemplating this path to a career.

Learning about floral design has meant more to me than merely acquiring technical skills. It has meant cultivating an awareness for beauty by visiting museums, dipping into art, and poking into galleries and also deepening my knowledge of plants by carrying field guides, visiting gardens, mooching about nurseries, poring over seed catalogues, and reading, reading, reading.

Never think that the last thing the world needs is another arrangement of flowers. As Ralph Waldo Emerson once said, "Flowers…are a proud assertion that a ray of beauty outvalues all the utilities of the world."

# How to Speak About Your Work

Recently I was browsing a website and came across the line "Shop the Story." The nuggets of narrative I'd just imbibed—about the founders and history of the brand—suddenly lodged in my throat. You mean it was all marketing? Yup.

Stories drive up emotional value and increase the price we're willing to pay. That "hand-harvested dulse pulled from the pristine waters of the North Atlantic" you're considering sprinkling on your eggs? Seaweed with a story. The flowers you reared from tiny seed to bodacious bloom, toiling day and night in your garden or on your farm? They have a salable story, too. So tell it.

That said, I feel a bit jaded about the story thing: stories that lack insight or information aren't revelatory. To speak meaningfully about your work, you need to develop a language, use metaphor, and engage your audience's intelligence rather than pandering to emotion alone.

In art school, students are taught how to present their work. They might talk about how they made the work, what it's built from, and their process of making it but also what meaning the work might have.

Here are some questions you might consider:

What's unique about this design?

What was going through your mind when you made it? Were you toying with a memory? Were you thinking of your client's personality? Was there a specific prompt, and how did you adapt it to the materials at hand?

Is there an emotion you were seeking to express? (Here, the hyperbred 'Super Green' ranunculus whipped up a fury amid the wilder flowers.)

Is there a greater story (one beyond yourself) you wanted to tell? Were you moved by a work of music or art?

If you had to describe the shape and form of the work without referring to anything botanical, what would you say? If your arrangement could move, what might it resemble? A dragon, a mouth, a clown?

How does the work speak to or represent its environment? How did you come by the flowers?

I could go on, but you needn't. Pithy does it, unless you are presenting publicly, being interviewed, or writing about your work and have to fill some space. Ahem.

Here's a great short example from Emily Thompson, who studied sculpture before becoming a florist: "15' of pizzicato and crescendo, gnashing teeth and sweaty palms this Election Day."

Picture it? I can. Distilled, words sear an image on the brain.

Having been both a participant and an instructor at floral workshops, I've seen (or been) both the frustrated and the exalted. I've witnessed happiness and delight but also tears and disappointment. With any intense collective human activity, there's bound to be some drama, and on top of that, flower workshops are both professional and expensive, so emotions ratchet up. Add the on-demand pressure of "being creative" in a group setting in a limited amount of time and things can get complicated. Here is what I've learned:

1.  Wear neutral colors or a single color. Consider yourself a backdrop.

2.  Find a friend, fast. Offer to take pictures for someone, and they'll return the favor.

3.  Don't take yourself too seriously; have fun. Don't you hate it when someone says that? I always do, but it's sound advice. Almost no one can manifest what they have learned immediately following a demonstration, and even your instructors will probably generate less than their best work under scrutiny and within time constraints.

4.  Take risks with structure but not necessarily color. You'll never find a more supportive atmosphere for busting out of old molds. The reason I'm cautious on color: workshop leaders will establish a palette because it's easier for beginners to succeed with a curated collection. New blooms + new color combos + new techniques = too many variables. Make color the one thing you can count on. Pick a favorite flower (or two) and build out a scheme from there.

Why Floral Design?

183

← Selecting flowers for a workshop is always a matter of balancing supply (dictated by nature) with demand (the spirit and style of the workshop). I was brought in to teach at Country Cut Flowers in Ontario; this beautiful spread was organized by Toronto-based Olivia's Garden.

5. There will come a point when you hate your work. Try to resist spiraling into private anxiety. Walk away from your design for a bit. Cruise around and see what others are up to. If you're really feeling the pressure, step outside or ask for a hug. Also, take a minute to check in with yourself: Have you had enough water? Do you need to take your work somewhere quieter? If you move through a list and find you're still struggling, then let one of the workshop assistants or instructors know. People are there to help you.

6. Finish your bouquet and centerpiece in a timely manner so your work can get in the photographer's lineup. You don't want to be last—not because the photographer will become less attentive, but the model may get tired and rightly choose to sit down after her tenth bouquet; more important, if you fuss too long, you'll miss the downtime you need to edit your pictures, post them, and prepare for the evening of socializing ahead. Floristry is about using perishable material well; that includes you.

7. If it's a residential workshop, avoid drinking too much and get some rest in the evenings. It's absolutely thrilling to leave your life behind and be surrounded by other flower lovers and gab, gab, gab. But do I wish I'd slept more the first night of my first residential workshop instead of dancing with glee, earbuds in? Perhaps.

8. Carry a pack or tote with a pen, notebook, water bottle, phone charger, personal whatnot, and absolutely everything you might need for ten hours on the semiglamorous go.

9. Trust that the universe will deliver the flowers you need. We all know the type that is first to the trough, elbowing in to hoard all the fashionable blooms. Let her/him. They'll find they don't need them all or their work will be overblown or, well… somehow it will all work out. As you now know, one of the key principles of working creatively is constraint. Too many

options can stifle creativity. You'll be faced with a vast buffet, so be grateful for limited options, appreciate what you have to work with, accept it, and begin. What you said goodbye to might come back, but in the meantime, you will have created something unique within a narrow range and you'll be on safer footing to innovate with flourishes toward the end.

10. Think through your exit strategy before it's time to leave. Do you have everyone's contact information? Instagram handles for tagging? The name of that ribbon supplier? Do you have a low box to place your vase in? Or a plan for carrying your bouquet home? Go into your final day organized so you're not scrambling or delayed upon your departure. You'll leave feeling calmer, more accomplished, and complete.

11. And one extra tip for the person who got you there: thank yourself. No matter what happens, I guarantee everything will change for the better after you participate in a floral workshop.

# Conjuring Mood

How do you want to feel when you look at flowers? Too often we forget to ask clients, let alone ourselves, this question. We might know what flowers we like or maybe what colors we respond to, but we neglect to consider mood.

Do we lack the language? Or have we forgotten the words?

Years ago I took a class at Zita Elze's floral school in London. One of the handouts contained an adjective list covering everything from appearance to sound, shape, size, and so on. As a writer I was delighted; the two categories of words that I found of particular interest were *condition* and *feelings*—those covering mood.

For example: *rich*, *tame*, *wild*, *tender*, *tough*, *prickly*, and *busy* are all adjectives that describe conditions. "I'd like something tame in orange and white, please," someone might ask.

A cat? But seriously, how useful would it be to have a repertoire of these adjectives to clarify meaning and desire? Immensely.

In the feelings department, we can use words to channel the ideas of others and critique our own work: an arrangement may feel confused, fierce, tense, exuberant, calm, happy, or zany.

Many in the design profession use mood boards to help plan events and decor. Pinterest is based on this idea of collection and collage, but making a pin board yourself offers a tactile and sensory pleasure. You can use images—cut or printed—swaths of ribbon, fabric, twigs, lichen…

Associative connections ensue: What does ice cream have to do, precisely, with that silk ribbon? Is it the color or radiance of summer, a condition of smoothness, a feeling of satiety or contentment? Memories and thoughts matter to mood. Perhaps that is the gift of flowers: to make us think *of* and *about* things, to create meanings and associations beyond what we see.

# Photographing Your Work

Seeing is hard. It's simply difficult to get eyes to do what they ought—open, interpret, and send a message to the brain. The brain jumbles everything—doubt slips in faster than a hungry rat, the brain creates meanings and associations, and, especially for the color-blind, sashays off in new directions entirely.

If people close their eyes in order to better taste or smell, what can we do in order to better see?

When I first started photographing with a DSLR (digital single-lens reflex camera), I wasn't sure what to expect. Like Harry Potter walking into Ollivanders wand shop, I didn't fully realize the power soon to be in my hands. "You can do great things now," I thought, but I consistently failed to do so. With my new camera I could do great things, but terrible things, too. Like try to make magic with shaky newbie hands. Like take sixty pictures that I was certain were in focus (they looked as much on my camera's teeny digital display), only to find once I uploaded the pictures to my computer that I hadn't come close.

A real camera is an amazing thing, but wield it wisely. Learn the spells from a professional. I hired a photographer to come to my house to assess the light. She stayed for three hours and taught me what the settings on my camera meant (at least, the ones I needed). I scribbled notes about camera settings while we tried out various looks in different rooms. Aperture, depth of field…This isn't the place for a full-on lesson about using a camera, but it is the place to tell you to invest in one.

That said, with every new phone comes a better camera; I know many a designer who creates beautiful work with a mobile (particularly

→ A giant mural sticker of a concrete wall forms a useful backdrop for this summer arrangement. Here, I've layered a slip of tea-dyed silk overtop. The plants include 'Hot Cocoa' roses, tayberries, *Impatiens omeiana*, dahlias, *Clematis terniflora*, *Eschscholzia* 'Thai Silk Appleblossom Chiffon', the leaves of *Begonia* 'Escargot', and a tuft of *Cotinus*. The United Kingdom's National Trust has partnered with a couple of mural companies to produce backdrops, so if you're looking for anything from old bricks to flaking scullery walls, you can order online.

in portrait mode). But if you have aspirations of publishing your pictures—making cards, calendars, or prints—you do need high-resolution images.

In this section, I'll discuss a few photographic techniques applicable to both cameras and phones to set you on your way.

## THE RULE OF THIRDS

The rule of thirds is the basic principle that dividing an area into equal thirds can help you to find an appealing focal point for any arrangement.

In photography, this rule might guide composition. Picture a horizon along the bottom third of a picture, with the sky spreading up above for two-thirds of the shot, as opposed to a picture where the horizon line sits in the middle. The former is generally more pleasing (see the Golden Ratio).

The rule of thirds also applies to verticals. Imagine two lines that divide a picture's width into thirds. In portraiture, a subject is often aligned with one of those two vertical lines. Some photographers even use grids in their digital viewfinders to help remind them of this alignment technique.

You can use the rule of thirds to position an arrangement for a photo, playing with the idea of negative space. If the focal point is the showstopping rose in an arrangement, it's easy to center it, but what if you place it off to one side? Would that better highlight its significance? How would the work appear with a wider space opening out above it? Or alongside?

I notice that when I photograph flowers vertically and post them on Instagram, they are presented initially in the feed as a rectangle (despite appearing in the grid as a square). This gives me a bit of wiggle room to play with thirds, either with the base of an arrangement sitting low in the field or above the halfway point if it's on a pedestal.

This style is reminiscent of the seventeenth-century Dutch painting technique as well as the bloom-heavy work of some Impressionists. Placing the viewer's eyes level with or slightly above an arrangement harkens back to this proven technique.

← A change of scene can work wonders for breaking out of old molds and pushing you to create spontaneously with new flowers. This quick lavender and orange arrangement of delphiniums, chrysanthemums, snowberries, and lisianthuses was born from a trip to the Utrecht flower market and a tour of my hosts' garden in the Netherlands.

### CREATING A VISUAL LOOK

No, this isn't about Instagram (again!), but it could be. It could be about thinking in blocks of nine images, curating a feed, and following a strict schedule for the release of your work: a close-up of a flower on Wednesdays; on Fridays an ensemble, flat lay, or collage; on Sunday morning a landscape; and Sunday afternoon—at peak traffic hours—a banger of an arrangement for all to heart.

Visual continuity helps set a tone for your work. While I may lack the self-restraint to pull it off, I do recognize it as a fine form of marketing (as do Instagram's algorithms: if you change your look abruptly, your post often tanks).

Not all designers have the time, talent, or inclination to photograph their work. Constance Spry used photographers under her strict direction. Sarah Raven has worked with Jonathan Buckley for over twenty years; Erin Benzakein's husband helps carry her visual look, as do the partners of the American designers Michael Putnam and Kiana Underwood. Lately, it seems it takes two to really tango, but if you don't have a person willing or able to help for free or in exchange for exposure, you will have to take pictures yourself.

(A short note on collaborations with photographers wherein you do the flowers, they take the pictures, they give you the pictures, and you cross-promote. Sounds like a fine plan until the flowers aren't in focus or the photographer takes months to send you the pictures or their look isn't your own. Worse still: if you do this with a series of photographers, the presentation of your work will vary considerably. That said, if you have a great relationship with someone whose aesthetic sensibilities match your own, a collaboration can serve you both.)

One means of creating continuity is to photograph designs in the same light and the same location. This is what I began doing in my living room, but I quickly got bored of my wall. So then came the backdrop variations: the mural stickers, which I stuck on foam core boards, the fabrics I then draped over those boards, and the hand-painted stretched canvases. After shoving all this gear into a corner of the living room too many times when company came over, I bought a backdrop system from a photography shop. It's meant to hold rolls of backdrop paper, the likes of which I don't use much, as I'm always spilling water, but I can hang swaths of fabric from it, which gets at least half the mess off my floor.

I have considered dragging old panel doors into my house and hanging windows, painting whole rooms, and, of course, moving to the country, where I could have a proper barn studio, not to mention a bigger garden. But, alas, I haven't had time to act on these ideas yet, so I've been making do and traveling to create new backdrops and lighting effects (which, in a way, is what stretches me most).

# Using a Camera as a Design Tool

Recall this image of old: A man stands in front of a woman, arms up, thumbs and forefingers at right angles to form L's. He makes a little box with those digits, peers through them, and says, "Oh yes! I can see it now."

How is it that when we see less of something, we often see more?

In floral design, we sometimes need to stand back and frame space to better see our subject. Framing is a means of tackling the questions of size, proportion, and composition. We often do it subconsciously, zooming in and out to make a problem more manageable, playing with scale to wrestle something to earth. We divide and conquer. We start small in order to go big.

Today, when so many of us carry phones in our pockets, we snap away easily, step forward and back, filter and edit and app it up. When I first began taking pictures of flowers, I used an iPhone. Not a newish one, just what I happened to have—a tool meant for communication and documentation, not art. As my work evolved, so did technology. That iPhone was replaced with a newer model that came with a better camera. Then finally I bought a real camera, a simple Canon Rebel—entry level, with an additional 50mm lens. That camera has taught me more about floral design than I care to admit.

First, it taught me to better see negative space, the area around your subject. That man with his hands up, peering through a box of his own design? He's deciding what stays in and what stays out. But more, he's looking for empty space, space that draws your eye toward the subject at hand.

Remember those black-and-white optical illusions that claim to reveal your personality through what you see first in a square image—a vase (in black) or two profiles (in white)? The lesson: we see the spaces around flowers sometimes as much as we see the flowers themselves.

Squint, snap, and decide.

Here the arching stems of *Clematis recta* 'Purpurea' provide line without mass, thus capturing space. Also pictured: *Dahlia merckii*, *Rosa glauca*, *Agrostemma*, thalictrums, 'Mother of Pearl' poppies, hosta flowers, and sweet peas.

# What to Read

Losing your mojo? Want to curl up with stories about flowers, color, or gardening on a winter night? Try these books.

David Abram, *The Spell of the Sensuous: Perception and Language in a More-Than-Human World*

Jennifer Bennett, *Lilies of the Hearth: The Historical Relationship Between Women and Plants*

Mary Rose Blacker, *Flora Domestica: A History of British Flower Arranging, 1500–1930*

Stephen Buchmann. *The Reason for Flowers: Their History, Culture, Biology, and How They Change Our Lives*

Mark Doty, *Still Life with Oysters and Lemon: On Objects and Intimacy*

Alexandre Dumas, *The Black Tulip*

Elizabeth Gilbert, *The Signature of All Things*

Jack Goody, *The Culture of Flowers*

Penelope Hobhouse, *Plants in Garden History: An Illustrated History of Plants and Their Influence on Garden Styles*

Tatiana Holway, *The Flower of Empire: An Amazonian Water Lily, the Quest to Make It Bloom, and the World It Created*

Beverley Nichols, *Down the Garden Path* and *Merry Hall*

Mary Oliver's poetry

Susan Orlean, *The Orchid Thief: A True Story of Beauty and Obsession*

Anna Pavord, *The Tulip: The Story of the Flower That Has Made Men Mad*

Molly Peacock, *The Paper Garden: An Artist Begins Her Life's Work at 72*

Eleanor Perényi, *Green Thoughts: A Writer in the Garden*

Michael Pollan, *Second Nature: A Gardener's Education*

Nori and Sandra Pope, *Color by Design: Planting the Contemporary Garden*

Sharman Apt Russell, *Anatomy of a Rose: Exploring the Secret Life of Flowers*

Sue Shephard, *The Surprising Life of Constance Spry: From Social Reformer to Society Florist*

Kassia St. Clair, *The Secret Lives of Color*

Amy Stewart, *Flower Confidential: The Good, the Bad, and the Beautiful*

Patrick Süskind, *Perfume: The Story of a Murderer*

# Life with Flowers

## MAKING BOUQUETS

Abundance is easy to fantasize about but a heck of a thing to manage. My first season growing flowers en masse, I had more flowers than I could possibly have dreamed of, and I needed a market, quick. Working with flowers—so perishable, and perfect for only a narrow slice of time—means you need to share the bounty pronto. My solution: selling bouquets at a local coffee shop.

I've continued this venture for a few reasons. One: my community supports me, and many of my bouquet clients are now regular clients for grander work such as weddings and other events.

Two: I can use whatever I want when I design mixed bouquets; I can cull the abundance, which makes seasonal and also economic sense—you lead with your strong suit, what looks best, and your customers notice that.

Three: making local bouquets educates people about the seasonal availability of specific flowers.

Four: if you're not social or you're busy with other things, you can drop and dash, leaving others to take care of the retail end and sell your flowers for a set price (I don't sell on commission).

Five: at a microfloristry level, as soon as you get in your car or van, you begin to lose money. So choose a convenient place that fits your aesthetics. I sell at a coffee shop–cum–specialty nursery frequented by gardeners and foodies about five blocks from my house. It's easy, and I feel good and grateful at every drop.

## BUILDING A BUSINESS WITH FLOWERS

*Concerning all acts of initiative (and creation) there is one elementary truth the ignorance of which kills countless ideas and splendid plans: that the moment one definitely commits oneself, providence moves too.*
—W. H. MURRAY

Working directly with nature demands flexibility. Before I started my company, Cultivated, I'd not owned a business. I'd contracted, freelanced,

worked for nonprofits and politicians (and tried to be one), been a student, and taught at a university for years, but I'd never stepped back and looked at how a business might fit into the landscape of my identity. I suppose there are many books about entrepreneurship that might have told me what to expect, but I still haven't read them. Perhaps I should.

What interests me now is responsiveness: how my flower business changes over time. What I don't excel at fades away, and what I need to learn or want to discover grows. It has happened organically: Cultivated's landscape has been shaped by my talents but also by which of those talents sell.

This makes everything sound smooth and easy, and it has been anything but. Growing and designing with flowers is hard work, not just physically but also psychologically—your plants are always on your mind. Weather, pests, and all the usual farmers' concerns nag at you; throw in harvesting and conditioning woes and flowers get complicated fast. You work at all hours, obsess over your phone, and scrub more buckets than you'd care to admit, but you work (in my case, happily) for yourself.

What's more, entrepreneurship, independence, pathos, drama, and creativity runneth through my familial veins. Flowers fit with this.

When I was writing a gardening column, I discovered flower farming and floristry; when I found I was creating floral palettes for designers, I began pursuing more design work of my own and stopped pimping my blooms. When I realized I didn't want to do many weddings, I diversified. When an interior designer approached me for prints of my photographs, I began to take my photography more seriously. When I couldn't cope with the garden's demands while traveling to teach workshops, I considered planting more perennials for cuts and hired an assistant. When my assistant couldn't maintain bouquet quality in my absence, I realized that I'd created a multiarmed monster—a business that couldn't do without me but that, like a starfish, can willingly lose a limb and grow a new one in its place.

What has worked? Being adaptable. And saying yes: to the odd event, movie producer, school festival, bereavement display, writing gig, party, interview, demonstration, farmers market, trip, speaking gig, and so on.

As you create income streams that aren't literally perishable, your flower business becomes more sustainable. So sell seeds, give lectures, print calendars, make jewelry from succulents, dry flowers, or dye ribbon with them...Do what interests you and try things that don't; they'll stretch you creatively.

Working solo with flowers means executive decisions may not always be easy, but they are yours alone to make. My business is so small that it's a wonder it can fill my heart. But it does—it allows me to be both home and away, meeting people who love flowers, too—and I dearly value the variety of my days.

# Epilogue

In my twenties, I made a pilgrimage from British Columbia to Findhorn, an intentional ecospiritual community on the open coast of northern Scotland. I went in winter—not a great time for plants, but they were there, everywhere, in herb gardens, perennial borders, greenhouses, and raised beds. All this greenery in a landscape so severe, so chilled by North Sea air, that the plants seemed like a miracle. Which brings me to the spiritual part—the founders of Findhorn claimed to communicate with plants, to listen to devas.

Now, I can't tell you exactly what a deva is, but Dorothy Maclean, one of Findhorn's founders, said that a deva is the spirit of a plant's essence. No spells or incantations were involved in her conjuring one up; devas respond to silent awareness and the willingness of a person to be fully present, listening.

I wanted to meet a deva, of course, but I lived about as far from great gardens and old-world spirits as you could get. At twenty-four, I'd bought some land and a cabin on a tiny island six hours north of Vancouver. The property sat high on a cliff overlooking the ocean and the mountains beyond, which makes the place sound more fabulous than it was, so let me add that I lived on a narrow lot of pure bush, wild, wet, and windswept, amid dense underbrush and gnarled trees. The cabin was sunk deep in the forest, rank with mildew, and had no electricity or plumbing save a pipe that drained onto ferns. Subtract the bush and I suppose the place wasn't so different from Findhorn—the soil sandy, the setting remote—but it felt very different to me. There was no amber sun seeping between lichen-crusted rock walls, no ancient footpaths, no hedges or stubbly, shorn pastures. My home was wilderness, in the truly Canadian sense of the word.

Margaret Atwood once wrote a poem called "Progressive Insanities of a Pioneer" about the lack of borders and feeling of isolation that such a place inspires. Now, I know Atwood didn't mean borders as in flower borders, but that's what I wanted—the cultivated and the tamed. I dreamed of beds choked with chickweed, a lawn brimming with dandelions, bluebells, and nettles. I might've set myself to weeding then, to discovery—a forgotten rose tangled in a thicket of ivy, primroses sulking under the shade of ferns, and pockets of deep rich soil left from annuals past. Plants might have spoken their history—a leggy fig searching for light or an old apple suckering up to the sky. With every chainsaw squeal, every stump torn from my ground, I yearned for a landscape that had been inhabited by someone, anyone, other than me.

The indigenous Tla'amin people had visited the island only in summer to dig clams, collect berries, peel cedar bark, and harvest the bulbs of *Camassia quamash*, burning back shrubs to keep those wild camas meadows clear. My property was no meadow, and other than some stumps that bore axed notches from the springboards of loggers, there was no sign of previous human habitation.

My ancestors were English and Scottish; my culture, horticultural; my orientation, retro-back-to-the-land. I was an environmental studies student and loved words like *permaculture* and *bioregionalism*—words that told me I needed to know where the water I drank came from (a spring on the island)—and words like *ecofeminism*, which called on me to act. If a philosophical education is meant to draw young minds into a higher realm of reason, what happened to me was the opposite; every word I absorbed made me feel responsible for how I chose to live on the earth.

I desperately wanted to garden. So my first question upon buying the place was: Where?

A rough deer trail passed through the property, and one February day I followed it—climbing over nurse logs, tangling myself in trailing black-berry, wading with arms outstretched to keep my balance as if I were in deep powder snow. Closing my eyes to avoid the snap of salal branches, I felt my way with my feet. Near the base of a hemlock snag, I stopped on a small plateau, poked my head out from the sea of glossy green salal, gauged the sun and wind, and pulled out my clippers. Then, I hacked. At first I produced a clearing from that heartbreakingly gorgeous salal; then, with a kind of savagery, I slashed and burned. In the fire, the salal hissed at me and spat. A towhee made catcalls. And I did not stop to ponder the importance of native vegetation—rather, I exerted myself against it even more fiercely.

I was on a reading break from university, so over the next few days, I worked myself hard—salvaged barky slabs of wood and hauled them and hammered them and carried in seaweed and scrounged topsoil from under big-leaf maples and finally planted a row of spinach in windblown sand.

I had a book about Findhorn at the time, and it inspired me, but more in terms of self-sufficiency than spiritualism. How could a dame of destruction want to hear from plants?

When I next went to the island, I bushwhacked my way to my plot and stumbled at the sight of a tidy little row of spinach, sparkling emerald in the sand.

But that one row of spinach did not a livelihood make, so after graduation I expanded that first bush garden—by dragging the cabin to the seafront bluff and designing a garden in its wake—and over time I think I expanded myself, too. I came to accept that it might be possible to communicate with plants: to acknowledge that in a particularly great garden, something else might be going on in the flower beds besides compost and wood ash.

I wondered what a deva might sound like. Would the voice of a beefsteak tomato be deep and raspy, the golden pear more seductive? And how did anyone really listen to a plant? At Findhorn, gardening with the devas was a form of worship, an open exchange between the self and the earth, a circle of nurturing capable of transforming an entire landscape. I hoped for the same. Yet if I'd heard more than a rustle in a breeze in my garden, I don't know what I'd have said back.

One day I went out to the garden to build a trellis out of branches. The idea was simple: a central branch of cedar for a post with smaller limbs nailed onto it, radiating out from the center. The effect I hoped for was pretty groovy: an eight-foot-wide rising sun coming up from behind one of the raised beds. I wanted it to act as a support for trailing nasturtiums (which climb) and to provide shade for the lettuces growing in the bed.

I collected the necessary materials: broken branches of red huckleberry and bitter cherry, silver windfalls of old red cedar and yew. I had a small handsaw with sharks' teeth, a hammer, and a pocketful of nails. First, I set the main cedar post into the ground. With some long nails, I fixed it to the slab of wood edging the bed. Next, I tried to artistically arrange the branches into a fan by securing them to the post, but after bending too many nails, I realized the huckleberry and yew should have been predrilled. I had no tool for that, so I found a way to wedge them between the other branches for support. I should have constructed the whole thing on the ground (which wasn't level, in any case) and then raised it like a wall over the bed. Instead, I ended up with two smaller posts on either side of the sun, which kind of spoiled the effect. But the nasturtiums looked happier for it, and though I couldn't hear them thank me, I trusted they might.

As my garden grew, I noticed there was always a to-do list in my mind with multiple levels of organization and a great hierarchy of needs. One morning in June: Sow lettuce. Transplant cleome. Weed arugula. Check compost…. Gardening year-round was a perpetual calendar with no end in sight. But visiting Findhorn taught me that all this was the little stuff, checks in boxes. Attention, really listening, was something altogether different. It meant loosening my mind.

One morning an eagle soared above the garden, circling over me with wings as long as my arms. It landed with outstretched claws on a branch. The tree shuddered, woke up. The eagle, thirty feet above, fixed me with its yellow eye and the point of its yellow beak, and I knew from the feathers standing on my neck that for a moment, at least, I wasn't thinking too much.

When the senses are awakened like this, who has time to deconstruct? Whose thoughts are not immobilized for a second by a backlit poppy or the flash of quicksilver caught in a lady's mantle leaf? With flowers, mindfulness remains just that—full to bursting with the singing reality of color.

The devas told Dorothy Maclean that "consciousness of beauty brings you into oneness, into any part of the universe," which sounds kind of flaky until you stop to think about it. It's true: if it weren't for the beauty of flowers, I might never have known what it feels like to belong to a garden, to really feel at home on this earth.

So what holds all this together—the devas, the flowers, the spinach, the soil, this twisting connection to nature so elusive and rare and yet so fine and accessible, like a thread? My garden needed me. Not only to weed or sow but to care. I want to think this is too simple a connection, that complexity could have better tied me to a place, but I created a garden that needed me because I think I needed that garden right back.

In the five years I spent homesteading, I grew up. At twenty-four I had been as wild as the land I sought to tame, and despite the frontier narrative of which I was a part and the environmentalism that made my peers block logging roads to protest the slaughter of old-growth trees, it wasn't wilderness that brought me closer to nature but a garden.

I went on to an internship at the Royal Botanic Gardens, Kew, in England and soon afterward sold my land. I still loved plants—knew their

206

names in two languages, their attitudes and inclinations—but in a way, I'd had enough of their quiet. At twenty-seven, I had a baby boy. We both needed a future with people, with words.

The verb *attend* comes from the Latin *attendere*, meaning "to stretch toward," and from a deeper root that means "to extend." That all fits rather nicely with mothering, flowers, gardening, and Maclean's ideas of attention: we tend and stretch toward understanding—we lean toward a greater sense of self.

Twenty years later, I sometimes still wonder about the devas and how if I'd been a flower I would have spoken to my younger self, for I know how much that woman was dying for a conversation.

In those days, she would have stood before you in pink carpenter's pants, her hair cut short, hands dirty, and told you that a nasturtium was round, spicy, and optimistic. The ridged pea of its seed, the creamy mountains and brown valleys, were wordless and thirsty. So she planted and hoped—poked the soil to the depth of her second knuckle, rolled the seed off her fingers, and saw it shriveled in a darkened hole. Squinting, it became a point of light. A possibility. Then slowly came the unfurling of a watery seedling, the split down a turgid stalk, and the tiny circles of green did speak to her as two true leaves came to hover an inch above the earth.

Silently they urged: grow.

And so she did.

This book is for her.

# Acknowledgments

The path to a book is a long one.

Thanks to Michelle Slatalla from Gardenista, who assigned me to interview Nancy Lawson, the author of *The Humane Gardener: Nurturing a Backyard Habitat for Wildlife*, and to Nancy for introducing me to her editor at Princeton Architectural Press, Sara Stemen. Sara met with me despite my having submitted a proposal for a book entirely different from the one in your hands, and it was her long-standing support that made this book a reality.

A year prior to approaching Sara, Erin Benzakein coached me on book proposals and told me the story of her own journey to publishing. Her encouragement and passion for flowers has changed my life, and for that I'm forever grateful.

I posted a number of the ideas in this book as microessays online @cultivatedbychristin and appreciated every comment and contrary position that furthered the refinement of my thoughts. Thanks to my online flower community and newsletter subscribers, whose responses gave me the confidence to press on. I hope one day we'll meet.

A number of mentors need to be thanked for cultivating my interest in plants and teaching me how best to express my thoughts about them. These include my dear friend the herbalist Heidi Schmidt; the ethnobotanist Dr. Nancy Turner; the ecofeminist Dr. Vandana Shiva; my first creative-nonfiction professor, Dr. Lynne Van Luven; my MFA mentors, the writers Joan Connor and Barbara Hurd; the farmer Caitlin Jones; and the environmental philosopher Dr. Duncan Taylor.

My friend and photo editor in the Netherlands, Joris Louwes, showed tremendous grace in dealing with my ignorance as a photographer. Thank you, Joris and Tirza, for years of warm hospitality and support.

Thanks to Frances Young, the Erskine family, and the Cambo Estate team for giving me the space to create art and share it with others; Danielle Dall'Armi for warmly hosting me at Rose Story Farm; Claus Dalby for welcoming me to his beautiful garden and home in Denmark; Anna Svensson for engaging with the section on restraint; Ah Reum Choi for her fine hands and eye; Xane St Phillip for reviewing the color section; Graham Smythe for lending me a vase and inspiring me with new flowers; and Aniela Woodward and Sue Donaldson for always having a strong opinion.

To all my students at the University of Victoria over the last eight years, thank you for teaching me so much about writing and life. And to all my floral design students whom I've collaborated with or taught throughout the development of this book, thanks for your kindness, curiosity, and beautiful work.

I'm grateful to Bayley Marion for helping me with my garden and business and to my father, Grant, who has rarely met an idea he didn't like to discuss. Thanks, Dad, for your indomitable spirit and engendering my love of publishing.

My deepest gratitude to my mother, Jane, who, before she passed when I was young, taught me to love words and the world.

Sarah Malm, Laurie Anne Myerscough, Paula Butler, and Penny Murray: thanks for listening, no matter what.

In the six months between book deal and deadline, throughout the life of Cultivated, and for seventeen years, my unflappable husband, Kyle, has given me tremendous latitude, comfort, and support. Al and Marcia: thanks a thousand times over.

Thanks to Christopher, our needy rescue dog, for forcing me up out of my chair and nudging my phone from my hands just when I needed it. You're a writer's/gardener's/photographer's dream.

And finally my thanks to Leif. Your success puts wind in my sails. Love you tons.

# Notes

p9 **You have no idea** Constance Spry, quoted in Sue Shephard, *The Surprising Life of Constance Spry: From Social Reformer to Society Florist* (London: Macmillan, 2010), xviii.

10 **When you write** Annie Dillard, *The Writing Life* (New York: Harper & Row, 1989), 3.

15 **The true secret of happiness** William Morris, "The Aims of Art," in *The Collected Works of William Morris*, vol. XXIII (London: Longmans, Green and Company), 94.

16 **For people who know plants** Amy Sanderson, personal communication with the author, December 7, 2018.

18 **The best flower arrangers** Penny Snell, quoted in Elizabeth Grice, "Meet the Garden Talent Spotter," *Telegraph*, November 28, 2016, https://www.telegraph.co.uk/gardening/how-to-grow/meet-garden-talent-spotter/.

22 **All these dried products** Gertrude Jekyll, *Flower Decoration in the House* (London: Country Life & George Newnes, 1907), 49.

24 **For how long have we** Constance Spry, *Flower Decoration* (London: J. M. Dent & Sons, 1934), 24.

24 **The hedgerows, the vegetable garden** Spry, *Flower Decoration*, 45.

24 **Provided the plant is beautiful** Spry, *Constance Spry's Garden Notebook* (New York: Knopf, 1940), 41.

27 **in a tall** Jekyll, *Flower Decoration in the House*, 39.

27 **flamboyant glamour** Matthew Dennison, "*The Surprising Life of Constance Spry* by Sue Shephard: review," *Telegraph*, April 2, 2010, https://www.telegraph.co.uk/culture/books/bookreviews/7544862/The-Surprising-Life-of-Constance-Spry-by-Sue-Shephard-review.html.

27 **Constance…has the supreme gift** Beverley Nichols, quoted in Constance Spry, *How to Do the Flowers* (London: J. M. Dent & Sons: 1954), 10.

27 **I want to shout out** Spry, *Garden Notebook*, 205.

28 **What is more irresistible** Gerd Verschoor, *Beyond Flowers* (New York: Stewart, Tabori & Chang, 1992), 20.

29 **Too many conventional florists** Fionnuala Fallon, Instagram comment, May 16, 2018, https://www.instagram.com/p/Bi281yRFqgC/.

31 **Name a thing** Starhawk, *Truth or Dare: Encounters with Power, Authority, and Mystery* (San Francisco: Harper San Francisco, 1987), 8.

38 **What cut flowers need** Sarah Raven, *The Cutting Garden* (London: Frances Lincoln, 1996), 49.

40 **Remove foliage and thorns** "Conditioning Flowers," The Garden Club of Brookfield, http://thegardenclubofbrookfieldct.org/conditioningflowers.html.

46 **One wants cupboards** Constance Spry, *Flowers in House and Garden* (New York: G. P. Putnam's Sons, 1937), 152.

55 **the shape was commonly used** Audrey Wang, email message to author, January 19, 2019.

62 **When you are learning** Helen MacDonald, *H Is for Hawk* (New York: Grove, 2014), 146.

62 **That I don't know** Thom Yorke, quoted in Austin Kleon, *Show Your Work!: Ten Ways to Share Your Creativity and Get Discovered* (New York: Workman, 2014), 18.

64 **For shallow bowls** Spry, *Flowers in House and Garden*, 153.

66 **The neutral colour** Jekyll, *Flower Decoration in the House*, 41.

72 **Colors change** Rosemary Verey, *The Scented Garden* (New York: Random House, 1981), 138.

74 **Each color is more distinctly seen** Leonardo da Vinci, *A Treatise on Painting*, trans. John Francis Rigaud (London: George Bell & Sons, 1877), 99.

76 **Nature is a good colourist.** William Robinson, *The English Flower Garden: Design, Arrangement and Plans* (London: John Murray, 1895), 223.

76 **The color we perceive** Kassia St. Clair, *The Secret Lives of Color* (New York: Penguin, 2016), 13.

76 **First, we must understand** Jessica Stewart, "Optical Illusion Goes Viral Because People Can't Believe What They're Looking At," My Modern Met, https://mymodernmet.com/lightness-illusion-explained/.

81 **It seems to me** James McNeill Whistler to Henri Fantin-Latour, 1868, quoted in Mary Ann Caws, "The Ethics of Translation," in *On Translating French Literature and Film*, vol. 1, ed. Geoffrey Harris (Amsterdam: Rodopi, 1996), 34.

86 **Luminosity is that attribute** Janet Smith and Anthony Gatrell, *Fundamentals of Colour for Students of Flower Arranging and Floristry* (London: National Association of Flower Arrangement Societies, 1999), 17.

89 **Yellow with magenta** Nori and Sandra Pope, *Color by Design: Planting the Contemporary Garden* (San Francisco: Soma, 1998), 11.

90 **In the case** Michel Eugène Chevreul, *The Principles of Harmony and Contrast of Colors, and Their Applications to the Arts*, trans. Charles Martel (London: Longman, Brown, Green, and Longmans, 1855), 11.

90 **incite each other** Johannes Itten, *The Elements of Color* (New York: Van Nostrand Reinhold, 1970), 49.

90 **Simultaneous contrast results** Itten, *Elements of Color*, 52.

95 **All my life** Spry, *Flower Decoration*, 52.

95 **At one yard** Pope, *Color by Design*, 11.

98 **The objects in front of you** Michele Cooper, http://michelecooper.blogspot.com/.

100 **In Latin the word for green** St. Clair, *Secret Lives of Color*, 209.

104 **The flower is charming** Georges Montorgueil, *Croquis parisiens: Les Plaisirs du dimanche à travers les rues* (Paris: Librairies-imprimeries réunies, 1897), viii, quoted in Laura Anne Kalba, *Color in the Age of Impressionism: Commerce, Technology, and Art* (University Park: The Pennsylvania State University Press, 2017), 55.

105 **Anything that isn't a color** Anna Potter, presentation at Perch Hill Farm, East Sussex, UK, November 1, 2016.

105 **Garden fashion depends** Penelope Lively, *Life in the Garden* (New York: Viking, 2017), 95.

111 **A regulating line** Le Corbusier, *Towards a New Architecture*, trans. Frederick Etchells (New York: Dover, 1986), 75.

111 **Let color make form** Charles Hawthorne, *Hawthorne on Painting* (New York: Dover, 1938), 26.

113 **Nature is perhaps** Raymond Williams, *Keywords: A Vocabulary of Culture and Society*, rev. ed. (New York: Oxford University Press, 1983), 219.

116 **Nothing sticks to a smooth surface.** Eric Weiner, *The Geography of Genius* (New York: Simon and Schuster, 2016), 193.

119 **Music played without gesture** Edward Rothstein, "Importance of Gesture in Musical Experience," *New York Times*, August 11, 1982, https://www.nytimes.com/1982/08/11/arts/importance-of-gesture-in-musical-experience.html.

119 **It just can't be** John Chamberlain, quoted in David J. Getsy, "John Chamberlain's Pliability: The New Monumental Aluminium Works," *Burlington* magazine (London) 153, no. 1303 (Nov. 2011), 743.

123 **When the whole and the parts** Samuel Coleridge, *Letters, Conversations, and Recollections of S. T. Coleridge*, vol. 1 (London: Edward Moxon, 1836), 197.

137 **Any great work of art** Leonard Bernstein, "What Makes Opera Grand?" *Vogue* (Dec. 1958), 159.

138 **The mood of the baroque** Margaret Fairbanks Marcus, *Period Flower Arrangement* (New York: Barrows, 1952), quoted in National Association of Flower Arrangement Societies of Great Britain, *Guide to Period Flower Arranging* (Leicester: Belgrave Press, 2006), 48.

143 **[Still life] is an art** Mark Doty, *Still Life with Oysters and Lemon: On Objects and Intimacy* (Boston: Beacon Press, 2002), 66–67.

144 **the soil proved especially suitable** Jack Goody, *The Culture of Flowers* (Cambridge: Cambridge University Press, 1993), 188.

144 **How many 'lives'** Donna Stonecipher, "A Poetics of Appropriation: On Sharon Core," Hyperallergic, October 17, 2015, https://hyperallergic.com/245428/a-poetics-of-appropriation-on-sharon-core/.

152 **Nature abhors a straight line.** William Kent, quoted in Horace Walpole, *Essay on Modern Gardening* (Canton, Penn.: The Kirgate Press, 1904, facsimile of 1785 ed.), 69.

158 **A flower…is never just** Lively, *Life in the Garden*, 49.

158 **An eye can be trained** Spry, quoted in Shephard, *Surprising Life of Constance Spry*, 182.

159 **I'm one of those writers** Michael Ondaatje, "Author Michael Ondaatje Returns to World War II Era with 'Warlight,'" NPR, May 17, 2018, https://www.npr.org/2018/05/17/612082798/author-michael-ondaatje-returns-to-world-war-ii-era-with-warlight.

159 **The thing you play** Ondaatje, "Returns to World War II Era."

161 **If you set aside confidence** Tim Lilburn, *Living in the World as If It Were Home* (Dunvegan: Cormorant Books, 1999), 73.

161 **Don't go against** Joan D. Stamm, "The Way of Flowers," *Utne Reader* (Jan./Feb. 2001), https://www.utne.com/community/the-way-of-flowers.

161 **You start a painting** Pablo Picasso, quoted in exhibition guide to "The EY Exhibition: Picasso 1932—Love Fame Tragedy" (London: Tate Modern, 2018).

163 **The truly fashionable** Cecil Beaton, interviewed by Dirk Wittenborn, "Sir Cecil Beaton: Photographer to a Gilded Age," *Viva* (Sept. 1978), 104.

163 **The style is the man.** Robert Frost, "Introduction to King Jasper," in *The Collected Prose of Robert Frost*, ed. Mark Richardson (Cambridge, Mass.: Belknap, 2007), 120.

163 **Style…is a relationship** Cyril Connolly, *Enemies of Promise* (Boston: Little, Brown, 1939), 12.

164 **test its flights of abstraction** Howard Jacobson, "Dramatic Speech," *A Point of View*, BBC Radio 4 podcast, December 29, 2017.

166 **revealing the doing in the done** Sanya Kantarovsky, "Muse: Pentimenti," *Art in America* (Sept. 28, 2016), https://www.artinamericamagazine.com/news-features/magazines/muse-pentimenti/.

168 **How do you exercise** Leonard Koren, *Wabi-Sabi for Artists, Designers, Poets & Philosophers* (Point Reyes, Calif.: Imperfect Publishing, 1994), 72.

171 **a woman could** Jennifer Bennett, *Lilies of the Hearth: The Historical Relationship Between Women and Plants* (Buffalo: Camden House, 1991), 104.

171 **Everything had symbolic meaning** Lina Krasnovaitė, "Language of Flowers," Filigrania, 2015, http://www.filigrania.lt/en/articles/language_of_flowers_article.

171 **was highly performative** Anna Svensson, email message to author, December 20, 2018.

174 **Wabi sabi is a beauty** Koren, *Wabi-Sabi*, 7.

174 **is comfortable with ambiguity** Koren, *Wabi-Sabi*, 28.

174 **The simplicity of wabi sabi** Koren, *Wabi-Sabi*, 72.

178 **Floral arrangement has historically been** Aniela Woodward, email message to author, August 29, 2018.

179 **Flowers…are a proud assertion** Ralph Waldo Emerson, "Gifts," in *Essays & Lectures* (New York: Library of America, 1983), 535.

180 **15' of pizzicato** Emily Thompson, Instagram comment, November 6, 2018, https://www.instagram.com/p/Bp2xFNWBusq/.

198 **Concerning all acts of initiative** William Hutchison Murray, *The Scottish Himalayan Expedition* (London: J. M. Dent & Sons, 1951), 6–7.

206 **consciousness of beauty** Dorothy Maclean, *Choices of Love* (Hudson, N.Y.: Lindisfarne, 1998), 129.

# Index

221

# About the Author

Christin Geall is a designer, writer, gardener, and photographer
whose work focuses on the intersections of nature, culture, and horticulture. Trained at the Royal Botanic Gardens, Kew, she completed
a BA in Environmental Studies & Anthropology and an MFA
in Creative Nonfiction before becoming a columnist for Gardenista,
a professor, and a designer. Through her company, Cultivated,
she teaches floral design in the United Kingdom, United States,
and Canada. Find her online @cultivatedbychristin.

Published by
Princeton Architectural Press
202 Warren Street
Hudson, New York 12534
www.papress.com

FSC
www.fsc.org
MIX
Paper from
responsible sources
FSC™ C104723

Printed and bound in China
23 22 21 20  5 4 3

Editor: Sara Stemen
Designer: Brooke Johnson
Cover design: Paul Wagner

Special thanks to: Paula Baver, Janet Behning, Abby Bussel,
Jan Cigliano Hartman, Susan Hershberg, Kristen Hewitt,
Stephanie Holstein, Lia Hunt, Valerie Kamen, Jennifer Lippert,
Sara McKay, Parker Menzimer, Wes Seeley, Rob Shaeffer,
Jessica Tackett, Marisa Tesoro, and Joseph Weston
of Princeton Architectural Press —Kevin C. Lippert, publisher

Library of Congress Cataloging-in-Publication Data
Names: Geall, Christin, author.
Title: Cultivated : the elements of floral style / Christin Geall.
Description: First edition. | New York : Princeton Architectural Press,
[2020] | Includes bibliographical references and index.
Identifiers: LCCN 2019014048 | ISBN 9781616898205
(hardcover : alk. paper)
Subjects:  LCSH: Flower arrangement.
Classification: LCC SB449 .G44 2020 | DDC 635.9/66–dc23
LC record available at https://lccn.loc.gov/2019014048